AF559997

JOB SATISFACTION OF SCHOOL TEACHERS

JOB SATISFACTION OF SCHOOL TEACHERS

By

Dr. Digumarti Bhaskara Rao
M.A., M.Sc., M.A., M.Ed., Ph.D.

Damera Sridhar
M.Sc., M.Ed.
R.V.R. College of Education
Guntur–522006 (A.P.)

DISCOVERY PUBLISHING HOUSE
NEW DELHI-110002

First Published - 2003

Reprinted - 2016

ISBN: 978-81-7141-652-3

Job Satisfaction of School Teachers

Published by:

DISCOVERY PUBLISHING HOUSE PVT. LTD.
4383/4B, Ansari Road, Darya Ganj
New Delhi-110 002 (India)
Phone: +91-11-23279245, 43596064-65
Fax: +91-11-23253475
E-mail: discoverypublishinghouse@gmail.com
sales@discoverypublishinggroup.com
web: www.discoverypublishinggroup.com

Printed at:
Infinity Imaging Systems
Delhi

Preface

Job satisfaction is a primary requisite for any successful teaching learning process. Job satisfaction is a complex phenomenon involving various personal, institutional and social aspects. If the teachers attain adequate job satisfaction, they will be in a position to fulfil the educational objectives and national goals.

Identifying the importance of job satisfaction in the life and career of teachers, a study has been taken up to identify the job satisfaction of secondary school teachers.

The secondary school teachers are having good job satisfaction. There is no significant influence of age, sex, experience, qualifications, teaching subjects, location of the school, and type of management on the status of job satisfaction of teachers.

The authors are very much thankful to Prof. D. Ramakrishnaiah, S.V. University, for utilising his literature and ideas to a large extent in writing the first two chapters of this report. The authors are also thankful to Prof. Padmanabhaiah, S.V. University and Prof. Ramesh Ghanta, Kakatiya University for their valuable contributions to the field of teacher education, which helped in preparing this report. The researchers, authors and teachers also deserve

the thanks of the authors, whose contributions are mentioned in the report. The authors are grateful to the teaching community for their services to the mankind.

As the teacher is the mother, father and God to a child in the institution, he/she should nurse him/her with utmost care and patience.

Bhaskara Rao Digumarti

Contents

1 Introduction

The successful running of any educational system depends mainly upon the teacher, the pupil, the curriculum, and the facilities. Of these, the teacher is the most important one and is the pivot on whom the entire educational structure rests.

Teacher was regarded as a holy person in ancient India, he was compared to a God. He is to be treated as a combination of the Trinity (Brahma, Vishnu, Maheswara) as well as the supreme ONE. Thus, teacher was regarded as the most perfect BEING in those days and teaching was considered to be a holy duty.

As per our Indian ancestors, the 'teacher' may be gleaned from the hierarchy of their Gods: *'Matrudevo Bhava, Pitrudevo Bhava, Acharyadevo Bhava'*. First, mother is God; second, father is God; and third, 'Acharya' or 'Guru' or the 'Teacher' is God. Further, it is said, *'Guru Brahma, Guru Vishnu, Gurudevo Maheswarah'*, which implies that the teacher is the creator, the sustainer and the ultimate liberator.

Centuries ago, in this Indian land of Vedas, certain principles which had something noble and uplifting about them were held steadfastly. These principles were emphasized in those famous verses in Sanskrit, which the teacher and the taught recited together and considered the essence of their mutual relationship; *"saha naavavatuu / saha nau bhunaktu / saha viryam karavavahai / tejasvi naava dhitamastu / ma vidvisavahai / ":* 'May he protect us both; May he save us both; May we do together great deeds; May our learning be bright; May we have each other'. Though the same lines are recited today, one does not always find the same zeal and the same enthusiasm. The teacher's image has unquestionably changed from an 'inner-directed' to that of a 'stereotype'. (*Ramakrishnaiah* and *Bhaskara Rao,* 1998).

The teacher was looked upon as 'Guru' or 'Acharya' and was given the top most position in the professional hierarchy. *Mukherji* (1957) stated that the teacher had no need to worry his head over the mundane necessities of life in the olden days, and hence he was free to pursue his quest for knowledge. In those days, he was a perfect model for the students in every aspect of life. He was totally responsible for the process of education. He was given full freedom in planning the curriculum, methods of instruction and evaluation. The student and the society used to 'look up' at the 'Acharya' for guidance and not 'look down' upon him as it is being done today. (*Ramakrishnaiah* and *Bhaskara Rao,* 1998).

Today, though along with other professions like medicine, law and engineering, teaching is also considered as a profession, may, it is said to be the noblest of all professions; people do not think of the teacher as a professional worker in the same sense, status and reverence in which they consider the doctor, the lawyer, or the engineer. A teacher does not enjoy a social status as is enjoyed by lawyers, doctors or engineers. Why is this so? It is because teachers are poorly paid and their income is low? Or is it because the majority of the teachers are from the poorer sections of the society? If so, are there no lawyers and engineers whose income is less than that of the teachers?

Or, is it because teachers have failed to impress the society about the importance and the dignity of their work? (*Ramakrishnaiah*).

Anjaneyulu (1971) pointed out that in addition to the loss of special recognition, the profession has been infested with a number of other evils. Enormous rise in the work load, lack of security of service-especially under private managements, growing indiscipline among the students and too much domination by the non-official political bosses are only some of the evils. It is no exaggeration to say that there was a time when ministers had to seek appointment with vice-chancellors to meet them. Now vice-chancellors queue up to see ministers and officials (*Subrahmanian,* 1987).

True enough, it is said that a large number of teachers of the present day have no interest in their profession but they continue in the profession only as mechanical wage earners. The facilities and incentives offered in this profession are so meagre that many of the talented persons do not think of becoming teachers but seek positions elsewhere. Lack of recognition of the teachers in this country is a very sore point. They have not yet been given the same footing as a doctor, a lawyer or an I.A.S. officer in the society. The significance of the role of the teacher is hardly recognised, though it has become a fashion to observe the teacher's day. The teachers of today suffer from neglect, indifference and insecurity. We always expect a lot from a teacher who has so little power and alarmingly meagre facilities. The net result appears to be a widespread dissatisfaction at present in the teaching profession as a whole. (*Ramakrishnaiah*).

Pagel and *Price* (1980) listed different causes for the dissatisfaction of teachers. They were: *(i)* lack of planning time, *(ii)* tedious paper and clerical work, *(iii)* an out-of-touch and autocratic administration, *(iv)* disruptive and unmotivated students, *(v)* non-teaching activities, such as faculty meetings and time wasting workshops, *(vi)* un-cooperative parents, *(vii)* lack of autonomy to prescribe curriculum, *(viii)* feelings of failure, and *(xi)* low occupational prestige. Therefore, a better understanding of the causes for job satisfaction/ dissatisfaction is desirable not because it will enable us to make them completely satisfied, but because it may help the administrators to relieve that intense and painful dissatisfaction which injures both the individual and the society in which he lives. (*Ramakrishnaiah* and Rao, 1998)

The Education Commission (1966) has very aptly observed that 'the future of the nation is shaped in her classrooms'. It is the teacher that moulds the most precious material of the land, viz. the boys and girls in their most impressionable period of development in the required shapes.

The teacher has a powerful and abiding influence in the formation of the character of every future citizen. He acts as a pivot for the transmission of intellectual and technical skills and cultural traditions from one generation to the other. The responsibility of the teacher is, therefore, very great. There is no gain saying, therefore, the nation's well being depends on the teacher's well being. (*Ramakrishnaiah*)

Saiyidain (1950) made the role of a teacher quite illustrative when he said that the teacher had to patiently cut, out of a crude and unshaped stone, a thing of beauty. His role, today, more than ever, has become exceedingly crucial in the national attempt to bring about several positive changes in the society, national progress and national integration. It is increasingly realised by all those concerned with education of children that the standard of education in schools and colleges has considerably fallen. In any scheme of improvement of the teaching and standards in schools and colleges it is the teacher who has a key role to play. Unless and until he is a fully competent person, greatly interested and involved in his work and does his job satisfactorily, all other efforts that are taken to effect any improvement in the field of teaching are bound to fail. (*Ramakrishnaiah* and *Bhaskara Rao,* 1998)

The University Education Commission (1948) emphasised the importance of the teacher and his responsibility. The commission was categorical about the need for improving his status, salaries, service conditions, and about providing facilities for the pursuit of knowledge and performing his duties satisfactorily. In creative work like teaching, job satisfaction remains the 'sine-qua-non' and plays a very significant role in attracting and retaining the right type of persons in the profession. (*Ramakrishnaiah*)

Job satisfaction involves liking for the work and acceptance of the pressures and aspirations connected with that work (*Anjaneyulu,* 1970). *Scheneider* and *Snyder* (1975) explained job satisfaction as follows, "It is most adequately conceptualized as a personalistic evaluation of conditions existing on the job (work, supervision) or outcomes that arise as a result of having a job (pay, security). It is the perception of internal responses (i.e. feelings)"

All types of work are not inherently satisfying. People engaged in the work which is not satisfying in itself naturally look for satisfaction from sources external to it. But job satisfaction does promote happiness, success and efficiency in one's professional activity. (*Ramakrishnaiah* and *Bhaskara Rao,* 1998).

Every profession has got certain aspects conducive for job satisfaction. At the same time it has other aspects that lead to dissatisfaction. Teaching profession is not an exception. If it is possible to isolate the factors of dissatisfaction, attempts can be made either to change the dissatisfying conditions or to reduce their intensity so as to increase the holding power of the profession. There is no gainsaying the fact that unless the teacher is satisfied with his occupation, he cannot deliver the goods satisfactory. (*Ramakrishnaiah*)

Statement of the Problem

"A study of the job satisfaction of Secondary School Teachers"

Need for the Study

Now-a-days there is a general feeling that the teachers do not have satisfaction in their jobs. There seems to be a growing discontentment on the part of the teachers towards their job as a result of which standards of education are falling. Is it a fact that the teachers are really dissatisfied inspite of the different plans and programmes which have been implemented to improve their lot? (*Ramakrishnaiah*)

Studies on job satisfaction seem to have begun with the famous Hawthorne studies conducted by Elton Mayo at the Western Electric Company in the 1920s. Most of the studies conducted so far are in industrial setting in examining the effects of physical conditions, design of equipment, etc. on job satisfaction and productivity. Elton Mayo and his co-workers started very much in this direction. During the course of their investigations, however, they became convinced that factors of a social nature also affect job satisfaction and productivity. The human relations school was thus born, which saw the function of the industrial psychologist as seeking to improve the happiness of the worker, and though this to improve productivity. The implicit assumption, of course, was that the satisfied worker produced more. (*Ramakrishnaiah* and *Rao,* 1998)

The traditional model of job satisfaction is that it consists of the total body of feelings about the nature of the job, promotion prospects, nature of supervision and so on that an individual has about his job. If the sum total of influence of these factors give rise to feelings of satisfaction, the individual has job satisfaction. On the other hand, if on the whole they give rise to feelings of dissatisfaction, the

individual is dissatisfied. Changing any one of the these influences will lead in the direction of job satisfaction or dissatisfaction depending upon the nature of change. (*Ramakrishnaiah* and *Bhaskara Rao,* 1998)

Locke (1969), however, emphasised the concept of value fulfillment rather than expectation. Satisfaction occurs when the job fulfils what one values. Just as expectations, values vary from group to group and between individuals within the group.

The progress and standard of any nation cannot be beyond the standard of her system of education and the standard of her educational institutions. The standard of any educational institution, in turn, cannot rise beyond the levels of its teachers. It is, therefore, emphasised by different committees and commissions that high quality personnel, who have the necessary aptitude for teaching and favourable attitude towards teaching, should be selected for the teaching profession. It would be rewarding, therefore, to identify the level of job satisfaction possessed by the school teacher. (*Ramakrishnaiah*)

Thus, the present study "A Study of the Job Satisfaction of Secondary School Teacher" is designed to analyse the job satisfaction of the teachers.

Objectives of the Study

The objectives proposed for this present study were:

1. To find out the job satisfaction of secondary school teachers;

2. To find out the job satisfaction of male and female secondary school teachers;

3. To find out the job satisfaction of science and social studies secondary school teachers;

4. To find out the job satisfaction of teachers working in govt. and private secondary schools;
5. To find out the job satisfaction of teachers working in rural and urban secondary schools;
6. To find out the job satisfaction of Graduate and Post graduate teachers working in secondary schools;
7. To find out the impact of the teaching experience on job satisfaction of secondary school teachers;
8. To find out the impact of age of job satisfaction of secondary school teachers.

Scope of the Study

Job satisfaction is a primary requisite for any successful teaching learning process. Job satisfaction is a complex phenomenon involving various personal, institutional and social aspects. If the teachers attain adequate job satisfaction, they will be in a position to fulfil the educational objectives and national goals. Identifying the importance of job satisfaction in the life and career of a teacher, this study has been taken up to identify the job satisfaction of secondary school teachers working in secondary schools of Guntur district. This study is limited to the variables such as sex, management of the school, location of the school, educational qualifications of the teachers, age of the teachers, experience of the teachers and the teaching subject of the teachers.

2 Review of Related Literature

Any worthwhile research in any field or knowledge requires an adequate familiarity with the work which has been done already in the same area. A summary of the writings of recognised authorities and of previous research provides sufficient evidence that the research is familiar with what is already known and what is still unknown. Since effective research is based upon previous knowledge this step helps to eliminate the duplication of what has been done besides helping in the fixation of useful objectives, formation of appropriate hypotheses, drawing of meaningful conclusions and making commendable suggestions. (*Bhaskara Rao,* 1989)

Citing studies that show substantial agreement and those that seem to present conflicting conclusions helps to sharpen and define understanding of existing knowledge in the problem area, provides a background for the research project and makes the reader aware of the status of the issue. Parading a long list of annotated studies relating to the problem is ineffective and inappropriate. Only those studies that are plainly relevant, competently executed and clearly reported should be included in the review of related research. (*Bhaskara Rao,* 1997)

The search for related literature is a time consuming process. Even then, it is necessary for a good research. Hence, this chapter is meant for the study and citation of studies related to the present study on job satisfaction of secondary school teachers.

The Teacher

Mukherji (1957) observed that four terms are used to refer to the teacher, viz., 'Acharya', 'Guru', 'Sikshak' and 'Upadhyaya'. It may be noted that the term 'Acharya' was reserved by Patanjali for application to the highest type of teacher, an original thinker and a master like Panini, while the other terms were used with reference to the ordinary teachers.

To quote *Gupta* (1973), "As teachers, we tend to forget that our roles are determined to a large extent by the expectation of the pupils". One might ask what ideals or qualities a teacher should develop and possess so as to fit in with his changing roles. One can not but recall the dictum laid down in the 13th chapter of the 'BHAGAVADGITA' about the characteristics of a real teacher: absence of pride, freedom from hypocrasy, non-violence, forgiving nature, straightforwardness, service of the preceptor, purity of mind and body, steadfastness and self-control. (*Rao* and *Ramakrishnaiah*)

The Teacher—Then and Now

The teacher in India has always been held in high esteem. Tradition has attributed to him certain desirable personal qualities which he will do well to cultivate in order to win and deserve that esteem. If the teacher is to secure and retain his rightful place, if he has to accomplish all that he might with his pupils, and if he has to find satisfaction in his work, he must know the qualities and qualifications required for the purpose and must strive to achieve them as far as possible. (*Ramakrishnaiah,* 1998)

Saiyidain (1950) made role of a teacher quite illustrative by saying that the teacher has to patiently cut from a crude and unshaped stone, proportion and balance. *Altekar* (1951) while explaining the status enjoyed by teachers in ancient India said that the teacher was paid the highest reverence by all people including the rulers. The teacher was called 'Guru' and 'Acharya' and was given the top most position in professional hierarchy. (*Ramakrishnaiah* and *Rao,* 1998)

Saiyidain further observed that we should take care to do nothing that will undermine the teachers dignity and self-respect. In this connection, there is a need not only for improving their material prospects but also according them proper social recognition which would cost the community nothing, except the cultivation of a better sense of values. and greater social sensitiveness. (*Ramakrishnaiah*)

According to *Apte* (1961), the teacher in those days was not confronted with any financial problems. *Mukherji* (1957) stated that the teacher then had no need to worry his head over the mundane necessities of life, and hence was free to pursue his quest for knowledge. But, today, the teacher finds himself handicapped not only by lower salary and lower status but also by longer hours of work and lack of facilities. (*Rao,* 1966)

Education Commissions

Many commissions and committees, appointed by the Government of India from time to time, have examined various aspects of teachers and forwarded recommendations regarding their status, salaries, conditions of service, facilities, etc. The opinions of some of the committees and commissions are worth mentioning.

The University Education Commission (1948), which functioned under the chairmanship of Dr. Survepalli Radhakrishnan, examined various aspects of the teaching staff and emphasised the importance of the teacher and his responsibility. The commission was categorical about the need for improving his status, salaries, service conditions and about providing facilities for the pursuit of knowledge and performing his duties satisfactorily. It further said that the success of educational process depends so much on the character and ability of the teacher. It opined that the success of a teacher will be measured not in terms of percentage of passes alone, nor even by the original contributions to knowledge, important though they are, but equally through the quality and character of men and women he has taught and developed. It was felt that the main cause for deterioration of standards of teaching and of discipline may be due to the indifference with which teachers are treated today by the public. Hence, due respect must be given to the teaching profession in order to the improve the standards of teaching. The commission also emphasised the need for providing the necessary facilities such as books, journals and laboratories without which the teacher cannot keep pace with the advancement of knowledge and carrying significant investigations. The conditions regarding provident fund, leave and hours of work should be definitely laid down. It stressed on the need for refresher courses for the teachers to help them have up-to-date knowledge. (*Ramakrishnaiah,* 1998)

The Secondary Education Commission (1954), which worked under the chairmanship of Dr. A. Lakshmana Swamy Mudaliar, also stressed on the need for improving the general conditions of teachers. The commission emphasised the reconstruction of the teacher in terms of his professional training and his economic status in particular and the status in the school and in the community in general. It laid great emphasis on paying adequate salary keeping in view the price index. It also suggested that other aspects such as working conditions, service, job security, leave facilities, work load, retirement benefits, etc., should be given for the teacher so that he can do his job more successfully. It further recommended that amenities like education for children, housing schemes, rail travel concessions, in-service programmes, medical facilities, etc., should also be provided. (*Ramakrishnaiah* and *Rao*, 1998)

"The future of India is now being shaped in her classroom" was the statement with which the *Education Commission* (1964-66), functioned under the chairmanship of Dr. D.S. Kothari, opened its report. It emphasised that to make any process of education a success, the quality, competence and character of the teachers were the most important aspects. In the opinion of the commission, it is necessary that intensive and continued efforts be made to raise the economic, social and professional status of the teachers in order to attract young men and women of ability to the profession and to retain them in it as dedicated, enthusiastic and contended workers. It also emphasised the principles of parity in remuneration to all the teachers with the same qualifications, doing similar work. It also said that provision should be made for promotional chances within the profession. It recommended facilities for accommodation and such other benefits for the teachers to attract and retain men of talent in the profession. The commission also stated that awards should be given at the state level and national level to motivate the teachers to do their job most efficiently. (*Ramakrishnaiah,* 1998)

Job Satisfaction

According to *Blum* and *Naylor* (1968), job satisfaction is the result of various attitudes possessed by an employee. In a narrow sense, their attitudes are related to the job and are concerned with such specific factors as wages, supervision, steadiness of employment, conditions of work, opportunities for advancement, recognition of ability, fair evaluation of work, social relations on the job, prompt settlement of grievances, fair treatment by employer, and other similar factors. However, other aspects such as employee's age, health, temperament, and level of aspiration should be considered. Again, his family relationships, social status and activities in organisations, like labour, political or social, contribute ultimately to job satisfaction. (*Ramakrishnaiah* and *Rao,* 1998)

Job satisfaction or dissatisfaction is the result of various attitudes the person holds toward his job, toward related factors and toward life in general. (*Gilmer,* 1966)

Job satisfaction is a complex phenomenon, as described by *Rao* (1970), having multiple inter-correlated casual factors: personal, social, cultural and economic. *Blum* (1956) also stated that a more comprehensive approach to the problem of job satisfaction requires that many additional factors—physical, social, temperamental and personal factors—be included for correct assessment. A theoretical view of job satisfaction as hedonic tone, according to *Blum* and *Naylor* (1968), may be summarised as containing the following elements. *(i)* The events or conditions experienced by a person in his job or occupation which arouse, among the responses, feelings or affects which he can verbalise on a continuum of 'like-dislike', 'pleasant-unpleasant', 'satisfactory-unsatisfactory' or similar evaluative or hedonic dimensions. *(ii)* People differ markedly in the degree of job satisfaction. In addition to errors of measurement, the variance in job satisfaction may be attributed to *(a)* differences in the stimuli, i.e., features of the job, and *(b)* differences in the job incumbents, *(iii)* The intra-individual sources of job satisfaction may be accounted for largely in terms of the concept of adaptation levels of the related concept of personal values. (*Ramakrishnaiah* and *Bhaskara Rao,* 1998)

Thus, there are many definitions and meanings for the concept of job satisfaction. To conclude, different operational definitions of job satisfaction given by *Wanous* and *Lawler* (1972) may be quoted. *(i)* Overall job satisfaction is the sum of job facet satisfaction across all facets of a job. *(ii)* Job satisfaction has been conceptualized as a weighted sum of job facet satisfaction. *(iii)* Job satisfaction has been operationalised as the sum of goal attainment or need fulfilment when summed across job facets. *(iv)* Job satisfaction has been operationalised as a discrepancy between 'how much is there now' and 'how much should there be'.

Motivational Factors and Job Satisfaction

Weitz and *Nuckolos* (1955) found that the decision to accept a new job would depend on expectations or anticipations of value fulfilments. To the extent that the expectations failed to materialise, job satisfaction would be relatively low and the likelyhood of quitting the job would be relatively great.

Herzberg, et al., (1957) pointed out that for people at higher occupational and or educational levels, intrinsic aspects of the job go up in importance while security drops off considerably. There is no doubt due to the greater 'marketability' possessed by the people in the higher occupational strata.

Crites (1961) analysed three relatively new measures of work motives and values and identified the following five arthogonal factors: material security vs job freedom, personal status vs social service, social approach, system, and structure.

Hackman and *Lowler* (1971) found that when jobs are high on the four core dimensions, (variety, autonomy, task identity, feedback), employees who are desirous of higher order need satisfaction (obtaining feelings of accomplishment, personal growth) tend to be treated by supervisors as doing high quality work.

Schmidt (1976) pointed out the importance of motivational factors like achievement, recognition, advancement, responsibility and work itself for job satisfaction.

From a motivational point of view, *Sergiovanni* (1975) suggested that over the long haul, external standards and impersonal control mechanisms and unduely programmed teacher activity and behaviour reduce the amount of discretion at the teaching level and also lower the amount of influence which teachers and students have over classroom activity.

According to *Schmidt* (1976), administrators are highly motivated by achievement, recognition and advancement in their profession.

Robert's (1977) study indicated that teachers ranked challenging work, good interpersonal relations, achievement of objectives, good wages, and fair and competent supervision as the most important of the thirteen job motivation factors.

According to *Davis* (1981), the primary sources of satisfaction of teachers were in aspects of working with students, intellectual stimulation, autonomy, holidays, and job security. Teacher satisfaction, according to *Daly* (1981), is affected primarily by objective feedback or individual perception as to the prevailing performance level of the school.

Karugu's (1981) study indicated that the Kenyen educators identified job security, sense of building the nation, chance to continue learning, love of jobs, love for children, extra-curricular activities, and communication with teachers, parents, and pupils as the most satisfying job factors in their current positions and also as the factors which cause them to retain their positions.

Kuhn (1982) found that satisfied teachers centered around intrinsic aspects or work, predominantly, helping students. It was found that satisfaction was a result of an achievement on the job, interpersonal relation and recognition; and satisfaction was likely to result in feelings of increased job commitment (*Hayeslip*, 1983)

Ahmed (1984) found that the most important predictors for teachers feelings of job satisfaction were the amount of pay offered by the job, the degree of help received from superiors, and the amount of say teachers had in decision making. Least important predictors for job satisfaction were found to be opportunity for promotion and the degree of fairness of work load.

Birmingham (1985) found that teachers were most satisfied with intrinsic reinforces such as social service, creativity, variety, and ability utilization.

Robert (1977) stated that teachers ranked challenging work, good interpersonal relations, achievement of objectives, good wages, and fair and competent supervision as the most important job motivation factors. In a study by *Hooker* (1977), it was found that authority and decision making were rated as being the most satisfying variables and compensation was rated as being the most dissatisfying variables of the study.

According to *Chen* (1977), the strongest sources of satisfaction for Chinese school teachers were: moral value, social service and co-workers. Prevalent sources of dissatisfaction were: advancement, company policies and practices, supervision-technical, compensation, and supervision—human relations. The subject taught by the teachers was also a source of job satisfaction.

In a study by *Marr* and *Mathur* (1973), it was observed that the largest number of teacher educators were satisfied with the fact that they found their work interesting.

Nature of Work and Job Satisfaction

The nature of the work done is very important element of job satisfaction. In fact, it probably can be said that it is the major determinant of job satisfaction. (*Ramakrishnaiah*, 1998)

Anjaneyulu (1968) study on the job satisfaction of secondary school teachers indicated that the factors which contributed to dissatisfaction were lack of academic freedom and heavy work-load.

Perumal (1969) also expressed the view that the assignment of any extra work to a teacher should be determined in the light of the work load; extra work should be assigned preferably to those who have the least number of periods of work.

According to *Gangappa* (1969), the multiplicity of tasks and duties makes one loose interest in his job and subjects him to all kinds of worries and maladjustments.

Clarke (1977) found that internal factors were more satisfying than external factors for most satisfied and most dissatisfied teachers. External factors were more dissatisfying than internal factors for both groups. Internal and external factors appeared to be related to job satisfaction and external factors appeared to be related to job dissatisfaction.

Work Environment and Job Satisfaction

It has been recognised that the work environment satisfies many of the needs possessed by the employee as an individual. The extent to which the various segments of the job environment contribute towards satisfaction of these needs, determines the job satisfaction of the employee. (*Ramakrishnaiah,* 1998)

American Vocational Association (1948) reported that more equipment in the Home economics department brought more satisfaction to home economic teachers. Similarly, *National Educational Association* (1957) pointed out that acquisition of teaching materials and suitable classroom situations were related to job satisfaction.

Rudd and *Wiseman* (1962) found that inadequate equipment and supplies as well as lack of other facilities have often been a source of low morale and dissatisfaction.

Rohila (1966) found that if the physical environment in which the work is to be done is unhealthy, it may contribute to a sense of uneasiness and that work done in poor physical conditions over a long period of time may result in dissatisfaction with the job.

Anjaneyulu (1968) divided the factors of dissatisfaction into three categories: strong dissatisfiers, weak dissatisfiers, and conditional dissatisfiers. The third group of dissatisfiers would cease to cause dissatisfaction if the situation was changed. Factors like frequent transfers, low standards of pupils, interference of politicians have caused conditional dissatisfaction.

Englhardt (1973) observed that job satisfaction of teachers decreased as the size of the class increased. Satisfaction also had a direct relation to the principal's considerations to the teaching staff.

Management and Job Satisfaction

The possible cause of employee dissatisfaction and low morale stems from the different frames of reference of administrators and teachers. This disparity is frequently conceptualized as conflict between the bureaucratic orientation of the administration and the professional orientation of the staff (*Blau* and *Scott,* 1962; *Etzioni,* 1964). A bureaucratic orientation emphasizes staff compliance with rules, regulations, and loyalty to the administration. A professional orientation, in contrast, emphasizes desire for autonomy and control over one's work environment and allegiance to one's subject matter and/or clients rather than to the organisation itself. According to this conceptualization, teachers are assumed to have professional orientation, where as administrators are believed to have bureaucratic orientation (*Corwin,* 1965). It should be noted that some writers have questioned whether all teachers possess a professional orientation and all administrators have a bureaucratic orientation (*Henson,* 1978; *De Young* 1980).

Stagner, Flabee and *Wood* (1952) found that job satisfaction was related to better employee-employer relationship. When the behaviour of administrators conformed with teacher's expectations of the former's role, satisfaction was high; non-conformity produced high dissatisfaction (*Bidwell,* 1959).

California Institute of Technology (1953–54) conducted a series of surveys of employees opinion and concluded that the employees expressed a great desire for information from management. *Suehr* (1962) also found that communication was one of the most vital areas in the whole morale process. It was most conspicuous by its absence, and consequently intended to be a major source of dissatisfaction. *Sommers* (1969) observed that most of the teachers felt that there was a lack of communication between teachers and administrators.

Anjaneyulu (1968), in his study on job satisfaction of secondary school teachers, educationists, inspecting officers, headmasters and retired teachers, found that in committee schools, the teachers were dissatisfied because of lack of job security, rigid and orthodox service conditions and too much of domination by the management; in mission schools, the factors were low standards of pupils, lack of parental co-operation and lack of right prospects in the job; in local board schools, the factors were too much interference by politicians, lack of social status and non-availability of suitable accommodation, equipment and furniture; in government schools rigid and orthodox service conditions, lack of parental co-operation and frequent transfers to distant places were the factors producing dissatisfaction.

Merill (1969) noted that both the elementary teachers and principals were equally dissatisfied with company practices and policies as well as with authority. *Butler* (1961) observed that degree of satisfaction was related to feeling of freedom or lack of it, that was allowed by the management in the classroom. The company or organisation was found to be causing the highest percentage of both satisfying and dissatisfying events with emphasis on money, working conditions, promotions, amount of work and recognition (*Locke* and *Whiting*, 1974).

Bernard and *Kulandaivel* (1976) found that the teachers of government aided private schools appeared to be better satisfied than the teachers from municipal and government schools. It was also found that teachers working under different managements had different problems.

Smith (1977) found that the satisfying elements in the principalship to be directly controlled by the principals themselves while control of the dissatisfying elements rested with the upper level school district management.

Reddy and *Reddy* (1978) observed that the teachers employed under private managements were the most satisfied while those in the government managements were the least satisfied. Similar results were obtained by *Reddy* and *Babjan* (1980); *Reddy* and *Ramakrishnaiah* (1981).

In a comparative study of job satisfaction, *Tabatabai* (1981) revealed that private sector employees were more satisfied with their job than public sector employees.

Chopra (1986) found that the teachers working in schools with open climate are likely to show higher overall job satisfaction than their counterparts in closed climate schools. Further, in open climate, school teachers exhibit higher job satisfaction in respect of two areas, namely 'supervisor' and 'identification with the institution'.

Security and Job Satisfaction

Security is one of the most frequently studied factors. *Blum* (1952) reported that security was less important to the better educated person, perhaps because there was not so much fear of lay off in the kind of jobs that the highly educated obtained, or the highly educated were justifiably more confident of being able to find other jobs if necessary. *(Ramakrishnaiah)*

Blum and *Naylor* (1968) made an observation that security contributes to job satisfaction, but cautioned that 'secure' is social as well as economic. Hence, it is believed that social security and economic security are essential to be happy in any job. *Kalanidhi* (1973) reported that the women workers in industry treated security as the most important job factor. Similar results were obtained by the *Fortune Survey* (1947) which stated that security for old age was one of the five factors significantly related to job satisfaction. In a manufacturing organisation both male and female groups describe job security to be the source of highest satisfaction (*Wills,* 1982).

Advancement and Job Satisfaction

Blum (1952) stated that opportunity for advancement was most important to sales, clerical and skilled personnel and least important to the unskilled. *Spector* (1956) assessed the impact of promotional opportunities on job satisfaction in a laboratory situation and concluded that meagre chances of promotion were causing dissatisfaction.

Herzberg, et al., (1959) suggested that job enrichment or vertical enlargement of the job are conducive to psychological growth of the worker. Regardless of advanced degrees and credentials acquired, in terms of prestige, a classroom teacher still appears to be one step above the student and one step below the lowest level administrator (*Bloland* and *Selby,* 1980).

Salary and Job Satisfaction

In this age of materialism and run-away inflation, man's worth is judged by the size of his bank balance, according to *Mishra* (1972). Thus, economic factors tend to over shadow all others. A radical improvement in the economic status will do much to attract and retain good teachers.

Anjaneyulu (1968) found that inadequate salary was one of the most common causes for dissatisfaction among school teachers.

In *Robert's* (1977) study, teachers ranked good wages as one of the most important job motivation factors. Similarly, *Shaver* (1977) observed that the biggest contribution among journalism graduates to job dissatisfaction was low salary. In the same line, *Schmidt* (1976) concluded that salary was highly dissatisfying to the administrator when it was not effectively present. *Roger* (1953) also found that the major dissatisfaction were inadequate salary, and factors related to the disproportionate number of women on the teaching staff.

It is very unfortunate that the scales of pay of teachers are lower than other categories of employees who possess similar or lower qualifications, experience and responsibilities (*Perumal,* 1969). He added that such a disparity promotes an unhealthy and undesirable competition and as a result, teachers become a disgusted and dissatisfied lot.

According to *Brown* (1973), an incentive is an objective goal which is capable of satisfying what we are aware of subjectively as a need, drive or desire. So, monetary incentive or financial need or drive is one of the most and primary motives of work. *Blum* (1956), and *Blum* and *Naylor* (1968) stated that in most of the studies financial incentives were found to be the most effective determinants of job satisfaction.

Counts (1978) conducted a study on public school teachers and found that inadequate salaries and narrow salary range between beginning and retiring teachers were among the principal reasons for leaving the teaching profession.

Eckert, Stecklein and *Sagan* (1959) found that low salaries was quoted as one of the three most common reasons for job satisfaction. *Anand* (1972) also found that salary was significantly related to job satisfaction.

But, there are a few instances where it can be observed that the influence of pay on job satisfaction is insignificant. According to *Mayadeb* (1972), salary was not the main factor which men, working in different positions as engineers, medical representatives and clerks, wanted from their jobs. *Butler* (1961) and *Ramakrishnaiah* (1980) reported no difference in the level of satisfaction among different salaried groups.

Sex and Job Satisfaction

Personal characteristics like sex, age, intelligence, or adjustment should be related to job satisfaction as work is an aspect of the total life experience. Hence, to some extent our attitude towards work reflects our personal history. (*Ramakrishnaiah*)

Studies on elementary and secondary school teachers, Chase (1951), and *Belasco* and *Alutto* (1972) have reported that women teachers tended to be more satisfied with their job than men teachers. *Bernard* and *Kulandivel* (1976) also found that women teachers expressed greater job satisfaction compared to their men counterparts.

Reddy and *Reddy* (1978) found that women teachers were more satisfied than men teachers. *Reddy* and *Babjan* (1980); and *Reddy* and *Ramakrishnaiah* (1981) also obtained similar results.

Female teachers tend to be more satisfied with their current teaching profession and they perceive a more favourable profession environment than male teachers (*Smith,* 1982). *Lewis* (1982) and *Birmingham* (1985) also found that women teachers were more satisfied with their job than men teachers.

Hollen and *Gemmill* (1976) reported that women teaching professionals experienced less perceived participation in decision making, less overall job satisfaction, and more job related tension than their men counterparts.

Gobel (1977) also found that women workers evidenced more dissatisfaction with work than did their men counterparts but they expressed more satisfaction with pay. Similarly, *Chen* (1977) observed that men teachers were more satisfied with their job than were women teachers.

Cohen's (1977) study showed that men and women teachers were remarkably similar, sex was found to be unrelated to organisational affiliation, job consciousness, degree of participation in the local association and degree of participation in the job actions. Similarly, *Atteberry* (1977) reported no significant relationship between sex and job satisfaction of elementary schools principals.

Among the university professors, it was found that either no significant sex differences in job satisfaction exist or that, it found, the differences are not psychologically meaningful (*Smith* and *Plant,* 1982). *Surbida* (1984) found that there was no significant relationship between principal's sex and their ratings of their overall job satisfaction.

Head of the Institution and Job Satisfaction

One of the most frequently cited reasons given by former teachers for having left the profession was dissatisfaction with their principals, according to *Browning* (1963) and *Yuskiewicy* and *Donaldson* (1972).

Sommers (1969) reported that the principal is the most important determinant of teacher morale. *Englhardt* (1973) found that satisfaction had a direct relation to principal's consideration to the teaching staff. According to *Ahuja* (1976), dissatisfaction increases when one has to work under an incapable, inefficient and indifferent head or boss.

According to *Bloland* and *Selby* (1980), an important factor in teacher career change is dissatisfaction with the principals which may stem in part from the principal's role often unintentional, in reducing or eliminating teacher opportunity for creativity in the classroom. *Lipham, et al* (1982) found that the staff perceptions of principal's leadership was significantly and positively related to job satisfaction.

Teacher satisfaction may also be influenced by the perceived ability of the principal to provide rewards for high quality teaching performance (*Daly,* 1981). Teacher principal relations and interfaculty relationships have a great effect on teacher's job satisfaction (*Mokry, A.I.,* 1981).

A positive association was found to exist between the level of teacher job satisfaction and the principal's perceived level of aloofness (*Holder,* 1985).

Age and Job Satisfaction

Age is also one of the most important variables in exercising its influence on job satisfaction. But, the relationship between them is again complex as pointed by *Hulin* (1977) since it is confounded with job level, income, personal and family needs and expectations.

Neeraja and *Pestonjee* (1975) also reported that age was the important factor which played a significant role in the determination of job satisfaction.

Holdaway (1978) reported that both fact and overall satisfaction were related to age of the teacher. *Kentle* (1985) also found that age was significantly related to job satisfaction.

Hull and *Kolstad* (1942) observed the results of several investigations and concluded that job satisfaction was relatively high at the start, dropped slowly to the fifth or eighth year, then raised again with more time on the job. The highest morale was reached after the twentieth year. *Herzberg, et al.,*

(1957) reported that, in general, job satisfaction was high among young workers, low among middle aged employees and it would increase again after the middle age.

Sinha and *Sharma* (1962) and *Anand* (1972) observed a significant relationship between age and job satisfaction. *Altimus* and *Tersine* (1973) found that younger workers were significantly lower in satisfaction with work, esteem, and self actualisation.

Morky (1981) found that the young female teachers begin their job with enthusiasm, hope and satisfaction and older female teachers end up with feeling of frustration, disappointment and dissatisfaction, where as young male teachers begin their job with low or average feelings of satisfaction and end up with a some what better level of satisfaction.

Belasco and *Alutto's* (1972) study indicated that the most satisfied teachers tended to be older in teaching in the elementary school. Similar results were obtained by *Smith* (1982) and *Al-Khaldi* (1983). *Birmingham* (1985) also observed that teachers over 55 years of age and under 25 were the most satisfied.

But, *Rao* (1970), *Pestonjee* and *Singh* (1973), *Anand* (1977) reported that there was no significant relationships between age and job satisfaction of workers. *Surbida* (1984) also observed that there, was no significant relationship between principal's ages and their ratings of their overall job satisfaction.

Experience and Job Satisfaction

According to *Siegel* (1969), job experience is related to satisfaction in a rather interesting fashion. As one might expect, new employees tend to be relatively well satisfied with their jobs. This 'honeymoon', however, terminates after a period of time unless the worker feels that he is making a rather steady progress towards the satisfaction of his occupational and social needs. (*Ramakrishnaiah*)

Neeraja and *Pestonjee* (1975) found that job satisfaction increased with increasing experience for a period of 10 years and after that it started going down. *Hodge* (1977) observed that the level of job satisfaction increased for professors as years of employment at the institutions increased in number.

Weinroth (1977) indicated that experienced teachers, over 55 years of age, with older children, had lower motivation and higher job satisfaction in the intrinsic area compared to 1 the young, childless inexperienced teachers, and 2 older, experienced teachers with school aged children. Young inexperienced teachers with pre-school children wanted less work pressure and were less satisfied with the amount of pressure on the job than older experienced teachers with school-aged children. *Lewis* (1982) also found that teachers who had continuous experience in the current school were more satisfied than others.

But, *Rao* (1970) found that there was no association between job satisfaction and experience. *Anand* (1977) and *Ramakrishnaiah* (1980) pointed out that the years of experience possessed by teachers had no role to play in the determination of job satisfaction. No significant relationship existed between the number of years served as a principal and ratings of subjects and their overall job satisfaction (*Surbida,* 1984).

3 Research Methodology

Design is the heart of research. The following aspects have been discussed in detail which are concerned with the design of the present study entitled *"A Study of the Job Satisfaction of Secondary School Teachers"*. The research procedure includes the operational definitions of the different terms used, the various hypotheses that were framed for verification in the present study and the rational of these hypotheses. The selection of sample includes the sampling techniques used, the reasons for selection of a particular sampling technique and the selection of the sample according to different variables. The selection of tools includes the selection of suitable tool for collection of data and the procedure followed in administerting the tool to collect the data required for the present study.

Taking the objectives into consideration the following variables were selected for the present study: *(i)* social studies vs science teachers, *(ii)* male vs female teachers, *(iii)* government school vs private school teachers, *(iv)* urban teachers vs rural teachers, *(v)* Graduate teachers vs Post graduate teachers, *(vi)* high experienced vs low experienced teachers, and *(vii)* older teachers vs younger teachers.

The population for the present study consisted of teachers working in secondary schools in Guntur district.

After a detailed study of the different sampling techniques, the stratified sampling technique was used for selection of sample.

OPERATIONAL DEFINITIONS OF KEY TERMS

Job Satisfaction

Job satisfaction is the result of various attitudes possessed by an employee (*Blum* and *Naylor*, 1968). In a narrow sense, their attitudes are related to the job and are concerned with such specific factors as: *(i)* wages, *(ii)* supervision, *(iii)* steadiness of employment, *(iv)* conditions of work, *(v)* opportunities for advancement, *(vi)* recognition of ability, *(vii)* fair evaluation of work, *(viii)* social relations on the job, *(ix)* prompt settlement of grievances, *(x)* fair treatment by employer, and *(xi)* other similar factors. Other aspects such as employee's age, health, temperament, and level of aspirations should also be considered. Again, his family relationships, social status, activities in other organisations—labour, political or social contribute ultimately to his job satisfaction.

In a study on job satisfaction, *Hoppock* (1935) proposed the following six major components of job satisfaction: *(i)* the way the individual reacts to unpleasant situation, *(ii)* the facility with which he adjusts himself to other persons, *(iii)* his relative status in the social and economic group with which he identified himself, *(iv)* the nature of the work in relation to his abilities, interests, and preparation for the job, *(v)* security, and *(vi)* loyalty.

Vroom (1964) listed the following seven dimensions which go into job satisfaction: *(a)* Attitude towards the company and company management, *(b)* Attitude towards promotional opportunities, *(c)* Attitude towards job content, *(d)* Attitude towards supervision, *(e)* Attitude towards financial rewards. *(f)* Attitude towards working conditions, and *(g)* Attitude towards co-workers.

According to *Katzel* (1964) job satisfaction is the verbal expression of an incumbent's evaluation of his job. In short, job satisfaction is an attitude which is the result of many specific attitudes in three areas, viz., specific job factors, individual characteristics and group relationships outside the job.

Job Satisfaction Questionnaire

Job satisfaction is the result of various attitudes possessed by an employee towards his job. It is the outcome of attitudes connected to wages, conditions of work promotion opportunities, fair treatment by employers, etc. To measure the job satisfaction of employment one needs a job satisfaction questionnaire. The present job satisfaction questionnaire developed by Dr. Pramod Kumar and Prof. D.N. Mutha measures the job satisfaction of secondary school teachers.

Science Teachers

The teachers who teach physical science and biological science were considered as science teachers.

Social Studies Teachers

The teachers who teach social studies were considered as social studies teachers.

Age

The actual age of the secondary school teachers was taken into consideration and categorised into different age groups.

Experience

The length of teaching a subject was considered as the experience of the teacher.

Qualification

The teachers with graduate degrees were considered as graduate teachers, and the teachers with Post-graduate degrees were considered as Post-graduate teachers though they were teaching at the same level.

Private Schools

The schools managed by private organisations or individuals, either partially or totally, were included in private schools. The public schools, government recognised and aided schools were also included under private schools.

Government Schools

The schools under the sole management of government officials were included under government schools. The schools managed by zilla parishads, municipalities, and government were included in this category.

Urban Schools

The schools located in an urban area (municipalities and corporations) were considered as urban schools.

Rural Schools

The schools located in rural area (panchayat villages) were considered as rural schools.

VARIABLES OF THE STUDY

The variables considered for the present study were: (i) sex, (ii) government and private school teachers, (iii) science and social studies teachers, (iv) Graduate and Post-graduate teachers, (v) rural and urban school teachers, (vi) age, and (vii) experience.

The rationale for choosing the above stated variables is discussed herewith.

Sex

As many researches identified a difference in the performance of men and women teachers, both sexes were included in the study to find out whether there is any significant difference between men and women teachers with regard to the level of their job satisfaction.

Government Versus Private School Teachers

Government school teachers are recruited by the state government. They can be transferred to any school in the state. All service conditions like pension, provident fund, retirement benefits, etc., are enjoyed by the state government teachers. Their promotions are made on the basis of a seniority list prepared by government. They have a greater scope for promotion to higher posts compared to teachers working under private managements.

Private schools are managed by private bodies. Appointment of teachers to these schools are naturally made by the board of management of the schools. There is no question of transfer of teachers. The work and conduct of the teachers in these schools will be closely observed by the management. Possibilities for promotion, needless to point out, will be very limited.

Science Versus Social Studies Teachers

The education, orientation, work, etc., differ in teaching science and social studies. Because of this reason, the science teachers and social studies teachers were taken as variables to identify the level of job satisfaction prevailing in them.

Rural Versus Urban School Teachers

The urban school teachers will have more facilities in many aspects when compared with the rural school teachers. Good atmosphere which is suitable to teaching learning process, libraries, science fairs, exhibitions, workshops, current trends in teaching learning process, etc., will be available abundantly in urban schools. A comparison between rural and urban school teachers will bring out the difference in the level of job satisfaction, if there is any.

Graduate Versus Post-graduate Teachers

While graduation in the concerned subject is the minimum required qualification for the secondary school teachers, some have other high qualifications as well. While the first group who have the minimum required qualification may be designated as suitably qualified, the other group may be called over qualified. Will variations in the level of qualification (suitable/over) bring about variations in the level of job satisfaction? To prove this, qualification was included as a variable in the study.

Age

Because of existence of contradictory research results about the relationship between age and job satisfaction, it was decided to include age as one of the variables in the present investigation.

The teachers were divided into 4 categories basing on their age.

Group 1: The teachers with below 30 years

Group 2: The teachers in between 31–40 years

Group 3: The teachers in between 41–50 years

Group 4: The teachers with more than 50 years.

Experience

The number of years the individual has worked as a teacher may have an influence on his job satisfaction. Hence, the teachers were divided into three groups depending on their school teaching experience.

1. The teachers, who have below 10 years experience were categorised as low experience teachers.

2. The teachers, who have 11–20 years experience were categorised as average experience teachers.

3. The teachers who have more than 21 years experience were categorised as high experience teachers.

HYPOTHESES OF THE STUDY

The following hypotheses were formulated based on the variables and objectives of the study. These were stated in null hypothesis form as "A null hypothesis states that there is no significant difference or relationship between two or more parameters. It concerns a judgement as to whether apparent differences or relationships are true differences or relationships or whether they merely result from sampling error". (*Best*)

Hypothesis 1

The secondary school teachers are not satisfied with their job.

Hypothesis 2

The male and female teachers do not differ significantly in the level of their job satisfaction.

Hypothesis 3

The science and social studies teachers do not differ significantly in the level of their job satisfaction.

Hypothesis 4

The teachers working in government and private schools do not differ significantly in the level of their job satisfaction.

Hypothesis 5

The teachers working in rural and urban schools do not differ significantly in the level of their job satisfaction.

Hypothesis 6

The teachers with Under-graduate and Post-graduate degrees do not differ significantly in the level of their job satisfaction.

Hypothesis 7

The teachers with low, average and high teaching experience do not differ significantly in the level of their job satisfaction.

Hypothesis 8

The teachers with different ages do not differ significantly in the level of their job satisfaction.

SELECTION OF SAMPLE

After finalising the variables of the present study, consideration was given to whether the entire population is to be made the subject for data collection or a particular group is to be selected as representative of the whole population. The 'entire population' here refers to all the science and social studies teachers working in secondary schools of Guntur district.

Of the above two techniques, the selection of a group as a representative of the whole population was found to be more convenient and suitable. This technique leads to a considerable save of time, effort and finance. The number of teachers selected will be small, and so it is possible to make a detailed and intensive study. This generally leads to more accurate and reliable results. As this sampling technique has many advantages, it was selected for the collection of data.

In any social research, various methods are utilised for selection and drawing of samples. After a detailed study of all these methods and considering the variables selected for the research work, the stratified sampling method was found to be most suitable.

In the stratified sampling method, the entire population will be divided into smaller homogeneous groups or strata, and then a sample is selected within each group. Every sampling unit in the population is placed in one of the strata prior to the selection of the sample so that the sum of the strata is identical with the population.

Stratified sampling method has certain merits as a technique of sampling. Auckoff has rightly said that 'stratified sampling enables the researcher to make a composition of properties of the strata as well as to estimate population characteristics'.

In this stratified sampling method, the investigator has greater control over the selection of the sample when compared with random sampling. In random sampling, although every group has a chance of being selected and included in the sample, there is every possibility, and sometimes it does not happen, that certain important groups are left unrepresented. But, in stratified sampling method no important group is likely to be left out.

Stratified sampling method is the ideal one when comparison between different variables has to be made. For example, if comparison has to be made between private and government school teachers or rural and urban teachers, it would be very difficult to select the required number of units through any other method of sampling. If any other method is used, the problem of bias and prejudice creeps in.

Replacement of units is also possible in the stratified sampling method. Normally, if a particular unit is not accessible for a study, it is difficult to replace it by another, but in this method it is possible. Stephen states that 'stratification automatically brings about a replacement of persons lost in the sample, by persons of the same stratum, thus partly correcting the bias that would result if there were no replacement of losses. As the entire population is divided into particular strata it is easy and convenient to replace an inaccessible case by an accessible one.

In stratified sampling method, much depends on stratification process. The following precautions were taken while stratifying the population: the variables involved in the study were taken note of; care was taken to see that each stratum in the universe was large enough in size so that selection of items could be done on random basis; the strata formed were definite and clear cut; each stratum was free from influence of the other; and there was no overlapping.

Before actually selecting the sample, certain fundamental principles were considered to make the sample scientific and clear-cut. (*Bhaskara Rao*)

Firstly, the 'universe' was clearly defined. In the technical phraseology of research, the whole population out of which the samples are selected is known as the 'universe'. For the present research work, the universe includes all the science and social studies teachers working in secondary schools of Andhra Pradesh. The study was limited to a particular geographical area, viz., Guntur district, to facilitate appropriate sample selection and to avoid wastage of time and money.

Secondly, decision was made about the units of the sample. A unit of sample may be a house, a family, a group of individuals or a single individual. A good unit should possess the following characteristics:

(i) ***Clarity:*** The unit should be clearly defined in unambiguous terms. This would make the study easy and efficient. For the present research work, a sampling unit is defined as science and social studies teachers working in any secondary school of Guntur district;

(ii) ***Suitability:*** A good unit should be well suited to the problem under study. Since the problem is a study of the job satisfaction of secondary school teachers, the unit selected is well suited to the problem;

(iii) ***Accessibility:*** The unit selected should be easily accessible to the researcher. If the units selected are difficult to reach and if he fails to make use of them, the study would be vitiated. The selected sampling units, i.e., teachers working in secondary schools are easily accessible since they could be approached in any secondary school.

Thirdly, availability of sample and preparation of the source list. This is an important factor that makes representatives selection possible. A source list is the list which contains the names of the units of the universe from which the sample may be selected. It may exit even before the beginning of the project or it may be prepared afresh by the investigator himself. Without a source list, study through sampling method is not possible. For the present research work, a source list, consisting of the names of secondary schools in the Guntur district is used. Care was taken to see that the source list was up-to-date and valid and that there was no repetition of names of the schools. This source list was found to be relevant and suitable because it included secondary schools as the study deals with the job satisfaction of secondary school teachers.

Besides considering these principles, it is extremely important to think about the size of the sample to be selected. If the sample is either too small or too large, it will make the study difficult and the results untenable. According to *Parten* "an optimum sample in survey is one which fulfils the requirements of effective representatives, reliability and flexibility. The sample should be small enough to avoid intolerable sampling error". The size of sample for the present research work was decided after considering the following factors. (*Bhaskara Rao,* 1989)

1. Since an intensive study was planned, a very large number of samples was not selected. In case of an intensive study, very large number of sample was not so useful as it involves huge consumption of the resources. A smaller sample will be convenient.

2. The size and selection of the samples are also influenced by the nature of the universe. If the universe is homogeneous, even a small-sized sample may yield dependable and required results. If the universe is heterogeneous, small-sized samples may not be useful. In case of the present study, the heterogeneous universe was split into smaller homogeneous, and samples were selected from these strata. For example, the secondary school teachers of Guntur district were broadly grouped under social studies and science teachers. A sample was selected from each of these two groups.

3. The researcher needs to determine the number of the groups to be formed. In case the number of groups proposed is large, the size of the samples shall have to be large so that every group should be of proper size and suit the requirements of the study. In case the number of groups proposed is small, even small-sized samples can fulfil the requirement. In case of the present study, the

universe was divided into male and female teachers, government and private school teachers, science and social studies teachers, etc., Since the number of groups were moderate a reasonable sample was selected from each of these groups.

4. Practical considerations and accuracy will also play a vital role in determining the size of the sample. Every study is guided by certain practical considerations such as time, resources, accessibility of the data, etc. Generally, it is believed that a large-sized sample is more representative and usually produces accurate results. This, of course, mainly depends upon the technique of sampling used. If the sampling technique is scientific, even small-sized samples can produce dependable and accurate results. While selecting the size of the sample for the present study, practical considerations like the availability of resources and time were taken into consideration. Care was taken to make the sample selection technique as scientific as possible.

5. The size of the sample is also governed by the size of the tools to be used. In case the tools are short, and the questions asked pertain to certain limited factors, a large sample can be selected. In case the tools are large and the questions complicated, the sample should be small in size so that, from administrative point of view, the researcher may not be put to unnecessary troubles. In the present study, as the tool selected belonged to affective domain a vary large sample was not selected.

6. The sampling method also determines the size of the sample. When random sampling method is used, the samples have to be large. On the other hand, if samples are selected through stratified sampling

method, the reliability can be achieved even with the help of the small-sized samples.

Taking these factors into consideration which influence the size of the sample it was decided that an ideal sample would consist of 80 secondary school teachers. This sample is small enough to avoid unnecessary expenditure and large enough to avoid intolerable sampling errors.

After deciding about the sampling method the universe selected was divided into different strata. The variables chosen for the study are considered in dividing the universe. The sampling design employed here involved not only that stratification of universe but also random sampling technique to select samples from within the stratum.

The total sample of 80 secondary school teachers consisted of men teachers—40; women teachers—40; urban teachers—53; rural teachers—27; science teachers—40; social studies teachers—40; private schools teachers—40; government schools teachers—40; low experienced teachers—17; average experienced teachers—33; high experienced teachers—30; below 30 years teachers—7; teachers with 31–40 years—17; teachers with 41–50 years—31; teachers who has more than 50 years—25.

SELECTION OF TOOL

A research tool plays a major role in any worthwhile research as it is the sole factor in determining the sound data and in arriving at perfect conclusions about the problem or study on hand, which ultimately, helps in providing suitable remedial measures to the problem concerned.

The selection and use of tools can be done in two ways. The first one is to construct a tool independently by the researcher for his own study. Here, there are many problems in doing so. On construction of own tools. *Anand* and *Padma* felt that 'A note of caution has to be struck when a researcher develops a tool for his study by merely pooling some items and does not subject it to the sophisticated techniques of tool construction. The result would be then, obviously, a poor quality research. With this, one can say that preparation and standardization of tools is a major task, and one should take care in aspects like selection of area and sample, pooling up of statements related to the area, consulting the experts and application of sophisticated statistical techniques. (*Bhaskara Rao,* 1997)

The other way of selection and use of tools is right selection of tools from already standardized ones available in the field of study. Here also it involves a tedious job in locating the tools and identifying their usefulness to the study on hand. Even then, this technique is very useful when a research work is taken to study in depth and when the research work involves a good number of variables. Some people believe that some of the instruments available do not measure up to their standards. Hence new ones. In some instances, consideration should be given to the logistics of the situation. Lacking time and financial resources for the construction of a test, many researchers cannot expect to produce a better instrument. In these cases, the most logical procedure that one can follow is to choose the best instrument available for this purpose. (*Bhaskara Rao*, 1997)

Considering the flaws and merits of the selection of tools in either way, the researcher is interested in using the standardized tool as the present study involves a thorough study of job satisfaction of secondary school teachers. Hence, the investigator selected the "Job Satisfaction Questionnaire for Secondary School Teachers" standardized by Dr. Pramod Kumar and Prof. D.N. Mutha to study the job satisfaction of secondary school teachers working in Guntur district.

Details of Job Satisfaction Questionnaire

Job satisfaction is the result of various attitudes possessed by an employee towards his job. These attitudes are related with specific factors such as wages, conditions of work, advancement opportunities, prompt settlement of grievances, fair treatment by employers and other fringe benefits. Job satisfaction may be defined as an attitude which results from a balancing and summation of many specific likes and dislikes experienced in connection with the job (*Bullock* 1952). The job satisfaction questionnaire has been developed with a view to provide an instrument to assessing the job satisfaction of secondary school teachers for applied and research purpose.

Development of Questionnaire

Initially job satisfaction questionnaire consisted of 40 'yes-no' type items selected on the basis of previous studies and following interviews with teachers and principals of higher secondary schools and teacher educators. These items were classified into four different aspects of job satisfaction in teaching. These included (a) satisfaction with work, (b) satisfaction with salary, security and promotion policies, (c) satisfaction with institutional plans and policies, and (d) satisfaction with authority including school management. These 40 items so classified into four different aspects were given to a group of twelve experts for their opinions and comments. These were also discussed with 20 teachers of secondary schools of Jodhpur city. In view of criticism and comments offered by experts and teachers, 9 items were altogether rejected, while others were modified or rewritten. Thirty one items were thus selected for the questionnaire. These items showed 100% agreement amongst the judges as related to job satisfaction in teaching.

First Try-Out

The teacher job satisfaction questionnaire, being a self-administering one, was administered to a group of 100 male and female teachers randomly selected from higher secondary schools of Jodhpur city. It was emphasized that no item should be omitted and there was nothing 'right' or 'wrong' about these questions. They were encouraged to answer each item according to their personal agreement or disagreement. It was assured that their replies would be kept confidential. No time limit was assigned.

Twenty seven items of the questionnaire were positively, worded and 4 items were negatively worded. All these items were scored '1' and '0', depending on the direction of the items. The sum of these values give the job satisfaction score for the subject. The total score varied from 0 to 31, showing lowest job satisfaction to highest job satisfaction on the subject.

Item Selection

All the items were scored out to obtain the frequency distribution. Twenty seven of the subjects with the highest scores and 27 of the subjects with the lowest score served as criterion groups (*Kelly,* 1939). Discriminating value for each item was then determined. Twenty nine items with discriminating value of 25 and above were finally selected for the questionnaire.

The Final Questionnaire

The Teacher Job-Satisfaction Questionnaire (TJQ) consists of 29 highly discriminating 'yes-no' type items.

Administration

The Job Satisfaction Questionnaire is a self administering questionnaire. The purpose of the questionnaire is frankly explained to the subjects. It is assured that their replies would be kept confidential. The subject is requested to read the instructions carefully and to ask the tester if there is any difficulty in the understanding of the instructions. It is emphasized that no item should be omitted and there is nothing 'right' or 'wrong' about these questions. There is no time limit for the questionnaire. However, it takes approximately 20 minutes to complete it.

All the items except 6 and 29 are positively worded. All these items are given a score of "1" for positive responses except for items 6 and 29, in which case reverse is applicable. The sum of these values gives the job satisfaction scores for the subject. The total score varies from 0 to 29, showing lowest job satisfaction to highest job satisfaction for the subject.

The sample consisted of 202 male and female teachers of the secondary schools of the Jodhpur city.

Result

The mean, median and S.D. for the sample are given in the following table. The distribution seems to be slightly positively skewed.

Table—3.1 Showing Mean, Median and S.D. (N = 202)

Mean	Median	S.D.
15.64	15.48	6.78

The skewness and kurtosis for the sample found to be 0.07 and 0.264 respectively.

Table—3.2 Showing Skewness, Kurtosis and S.E. (N = 202)

Mean	Value	S.E.
Skewness	0.070	0.170 ns
Kurtosis	0.264	0.058 ns

Since the S.E. of skewness and kurtosis is less than ± 1.96, the 5% level of confidence is interpreted, that the sample does not differ from normality (Mc Narmar, 1962).

Reliability

The split-half reliability (correlating the odd-even items) of the test applying Spearman-Brown formula is 0.95 (N =100) with an index reliability of 0.97.

The test-retest reliability of the test is 0.73 (N = 60: time interval = 3 months) with an index reliability of 0.85 (Table—3.3).

Table—3.3 Showing Split-Half and Test-Retest Reliability

Method	n	r-value	Index of reliability
Split-half	100	0.95	0.97
Test-retest	60	0.73	0.85

Validity

Only highly discriminating items are included in the questionnaire following item analysis (*Garrett,* 1961). The upper 27% and lower 27% served as criterion groups (*Kelly,* 1939). The face validity of the measures is very high. The content validity is ensured as the items for which there has been 100 per cent agreement amongst judges regarding their relevancy to teacher's job satisfaction are included in the questionnaire.

The Job Satisfaction Questionnaire, thus developed, consists of 29 items to measure the job satisfaction of school teachers.

ADMINISTRATION OF TOOL

The Job Satisfaction Questionnaire was administered on a small sample before finally administered and found suitable for the present study.

The tool was personally administered and got the data for analysis.

4 Analysis of Data

The next steps in the process of research, after the collection of data, are the organisation, analysis and interpretation of data and formulation of conclusions and generalisations to get a meaningful picture out of the raw information collected. The analysis and interpretation of data involve the objective material in the possession of the researcher and his subjective reactions and desires to be derived from the data.

The mass data collected through the use of tool need to be systematized and organised, i.e., edited, classified and tabulated before it can serve the purpose. Here, editing implies the checking of gathered data for accuracy, utility and completeness; classifying refers to the dividing of the information into different categories, classes or heads for use; and tabulating denotes the recording of the classified material in accurate mathematical terms, i.e., marking and counting frequency tallies for different items on which information is gathered.

Analysis of data means studying the tabulated material in order to determine inherent facts or meanings. It involves breaking down the existing complex factors into simplex parts and putting the parts together in new arrangements for purposes of interpretation.

The total score of job satisfaction of each teacher was taken to find out the level of job satisfaction possessed by each sub sample as well as total sample of the study. The maximum score that a teacher can get is 29 and the minimum is 0. In the present study, the highest score secured by a teacher was 28 and the lowest was 9.

For the purpose of a classification of the level of job satisfaction possessed by the secondary school teachers, the job satisfaction level was divided into five categories, namely, very poor (0-5 scores), poor (6-11 scores), average (12-17 scores), good (18-23 scores), and very good (24-29 scores).

The mean scores were used to identify the level of job satisfaction of secondary, teachers and to compare the sub-sample variation. The values of standard deviation were used to measure the spread or dispersion of scores in the distribution. The critical ratios were calculated to test the significant difference in the means of the sub-samples of each variable. The chi-square test of independence was applied for comparing the experimentally obtained results with those of to be expected theoretically on the hypothesis of equal probable distribution.

Hypothesis—1

"The secondary school teachers are not satisfied with their job".

To test the validity of hypothesis 1, total scores of all the sample were calculated to arrive at mean and standard deviation of secondary school teachers.

Table—4.1 Level of Job Satisfaction of Secondary School Teachers

Sample Size	Mean	Standard Deviation
80	21.8	4.37

The secondary school teachers were holding good job satisfaction. As per the standard deviation, the job satisfaction was normally distributed in the sample.

The chi-square test of independence was applied to test the divergence of observed results from those expected on the hypothesis of equal probability distribution of a trait in the sample.

Table—4.2 Distribution of Job Satisfaction in the Secondary School Teachers

Job satisfaction Category	Frequency expected f_e	Frequency observed f_o	Chi-square value x^2
Very poor	2.4	0	
Poor	19.2	3	
Average	36.8	7	446.85*
Good	19.2	37	
Very good	2.4	33	

df = 2, P at 0.01 levels 9.21 *Significant at 0.01 level

As per the chi-square value, the distribution of job satisfaction in the whole sample was not normally distributed.

The hypothesis that "The secondary school teachers are not satisfied with their job" can be rejected as the sample was holding good job satisfaction.

Hypothesis—2

"The men and women teachers do not differ significantly in the level of their job satisfaction".

A comparison of the scores of job satisfaction of men and women secondary school teachers was made to identify the difference in the level of job satisfaction possessed by them. The data as follows:

Table—4.3 Comparison of Job Satisfaction of Men and Women Teachers

Variables	Sample size	Mean	Standard deviation	Mean difference	Critical ratio
Men	40	21.0	4.32		
Women	40	22.6	4.26	0.96	1.67#

P at 0.01 level is 2.58 #Not significant at 0.01 level

Both men and women teachers working in secondary schools were holding good job satisfaction. The women teachers were having a little bit high job satisfaction when compared with their counterparts.

As per the standard deviation values, the divergence in job satisfaction scores is equal in both men and women teachers.

As the critical ratio value was not significant, it can be said that the little difference that exists in the job satisfaction of men and women teachers may be due to sampling error.

The chi-square test was applied to test the divergence of observed results of men and women teacners from those expected on equal probability distribution. The chi-square values as follows:

Table—4.4 Distribution of Job Satisfaction in Male and Female Teachers

Job satisfaction category	Men Teachers			Women Teachers		
	f_e	f_o	x^2	f_e	f_o	x^2
Very poor	1.2	0		1.2	0	
Poor	9.6	2		9.6	1	
Average	18.4	4	148.06*	18.4	3	320.59*
Good	9.6	21		9.6	1.6	
Very good	1.2	13		1.2	20	

*Significant at 0.01 level

There was a significant divergence in the level of job satisfaction possessed by men and women teachers. The divergence of scores was more in women teachers when compared with men teachers.

The hypothesis that "The men and women teachers do not differ significantly in the level of their job satisfaction" can be accepted as the men and women teachers were possessing good job satisfaction.

Hypothesis—3

"The science and social studies teachers do not differ significantly in the level of their job satisfaction".

To test the validity of the above hypothesis, a comparison was made to identify the difference in the level of job satisfaction possessed by science and social studies teachers. The data as follows:

Table—4.5 Comparison of Job Satisfaction of Science and Social Studies Teachers

Variable	Sample size	Mean	Standard deviation	Mean difference	Critical ratio
Science teachers	40	21.07	4.71		
Social studies teachers	40	22.53	3.85	1.46	1.52#

Not significant at 0.01 level

The science and social studies teachers were possessing good job satisfaction. When compared, the social studies teachers were holding a little bit high job satisfaction than the science teachers.

As per the standard deviation scores, the dispersion of job satisfaction was more in science teachers and less in social studies teachers though the difference between these two very small.

As per the value of the critical ratio, there was no significant difference in the level of job satisfaction possessed by science and social studies teachers.

The chi-square test was applied to test the divergence of observed results from those expected. The results as follows:

Table—4.6 Distribution of Job Satisfaction in Science and Social Studies Teachers

Job satisfaction category	Science teachers			Social Studies teachers		
	f_e	f_o	x^2	f_e	f_o	x^2
Very poor	1.2	0		1.2	0	
Poor	9.6	3		9.6	0	
Average	18.4	3	148.20*	18.4	4	320.87*
Good	9.6	21		9.6	16	
Very good	1.2	13		1.2	20	

* Significant at 0.01 level

As per the chi-square values, there is a little bit high divergence in the distribution of job satisfaction in social studies teachers when compared with science teachers.

The hypothesis that "The science and social studies teachers do not differ significantly in the level of their job satisfaction" can be accepted as both of them were possessing good job satisfaction.

Hypothesis—4

"The teachers working in government and private schools do not differ significantly in the level of their job satisfaction".

A comparison of the job satisfaction of private and government schools teachers was made to test the validity of the above hypothesis. The data as follows:

Table—4.7 Comparison of Job Satisfaction of Government and Private Schools Teachers

Variable	Sample size	Mean	Standard deviation	Mean difference	Critical ratio
Govt. teachers	40	20.62	4.68		
Private teachers	40	22.98	8.67	2.36	2.51#

Not significant at 0.01 level

The teachers working in private and government secondary schools were possessing good job satisfaction.

The distribution of teachers in different job satisfaction categories was more in government schools when compared with private schools as per the standard deviation values.

As the value of the critical ratio was not significant, the little difference in the job satisfaction between teachers working in government and private schools was not worth considerable.

The chi-square test was applied to test the divergence of observed results from those expected on the hypothesis of equal probable distribution. The results as follows:

There was a significant difference in the level of job satisfaction possessed by the teachers working in private and government secondary schools. There was also a greater divergence in private school teachers when compared with their counterparts.

The hypothesis that "The teachers working in government and private secondary schools do not differ significantly in the level of their job satisfaction" can be accepted as the sub-samples were possessing good job satisfaction.

Table—4.8 Distribution of Job Satisfaction in the Government and Private Schools Teachers

Job satisfaction category	Govt. teachers			Private teachers		
	f_e	f_o	x^2	f_e	f_o	x^2
Very poor	1.2	0		1.2	0	
Poor	9.6	3		9.6	0	
Average	18.4	3	104.76*	18.4	4	419.30*
Good	9.6	24		9.6	13	
Very good	1.2	10		1.2	23	

*Significant at 0.01 level

Hypothesis—5

"The teachers working in rural and urban schools do not differ significantly in the level of their job satisfaction".

A comparison was made to identify the difference in the possession of job satisfaction by urban and rural teachers. The results as follows:

Table—4.9 Comparison of Job Satisfaction of Urban and Rural Teachers

Variable	Sample size	Mean	Standard deviation	Mean difference	Critical ratio
Urban teachers	53	21.57	4.46		
Rural teachers	27	22.26	4.13	0.69	0.69#

Not significant at 0.01 level

The teachers working in rural and urban secondary schools were possessing good job satisfaction. When compared the job satisfaction of sub-samples, the rural teachers were holding a negligible amount of high job satisfaction than the urban teachers.

As per the values of the standard deviation, the distribution of job satisfaction among the rural and urban teachers was equal.

As per the critical ratio value also, there was no significant difference in the level of job satisfaction possessed by rural and urban teachers.

The chi-square test values of the teachers working in urban and rural schools are given in the following table:

Table—4.10 Distribution of Job Satisfaction in the Urban and Rural teachers

Job satisfaction category	Rural teachers			Urban teachers		
	F_e	f_o	x^2	f_e	f_o	x^2
Very poor	0.81	0		1.59	0	
Poor	6.48	1		12.72	2	
Average	12.42	2	173.47*	24.38	5	274.84*
Good	6.48	12		12.72	25	
Very good	0.81	12		1.59	21	

* Significant at 0.01 level

There was a significant difference in the distribution of job satisfaction among rural and urban teachers. As per the chi-square values, there was a greater divergence in the distribution of job satisfaction in urban teachers.

The hypothesis that "The teachers working in rural and urban secondary schools do not differ significantly in the level of their job satisfaction" can be accepted as the rural and urban teachers were possessing good job satisfaction.

Hypothesis—6

"The teachers with Graduate and Post-graduate degrees do not differ significantly in the level of their job satisfaction".

To test the validity of the above hypothesis, a comparison was made to identify the level of job satisfaction possessed by Graduate and Post-graduate teachers. The results as follows:

Table—4.11 Comparison of Job Satisfaction of Graduate and Post-graduate Teachers

Variable	Sample size	Mean	Standard deviation	Mean difference	Critical ratio
Graduate teachers	59	22.10	4.69		
Post-graduate teachers	21	20.95	3.12	1.15	1.26#

Not significant at 0.01 level

The Graduate and Post-graduate teachers were holding good job satisfaction. The Graduate teachers were holding a little bit high job satisfaction than the post-graduate teachers.

As per the standard deviation values, the distribution of teachers in different levels of job satisfaction was more in Graduate teachers when compared with Post-graduate teachers.

As the value of critical ratio was not significant, there was no significant difference in the level of job satisfaction possessed by the Graduate and Post-graduate teachers.

The chi-square test was applied to test the divergence of obtained results from those of expected in the sample on the hypothesis of equal probability. The results as follows:

Table—4.12 Distribution of Job Satisfaction in Graduate and Post-graduate Teachers

Job satisfaction category	Graduate teachers			Post-graduate teachers		
	f_e	f_o	x^2	f_e	f_o	x^2
Very poor	1.77	0		0.63	0	
Poor	14.16	3		5.04	0	
Average	27.14	4	425.85*	9.66	3	53.14*
Good	14.16	24		5.04	13	
Very good	1.77	28		0.63	5	

* Significant at 0.01 level

As per the chi-square values, the distribution of sample in various categories of job satisfaction was more significant in Graduate teachers when compared with Post-graduate teachers.

The hypothesis that "The teachers with Graduate and Post-graduate degrees do not differ significantly in the level of their job satisfaction" can be accepted as the Graduate and Post-graduate teachers were possessing good job satisfaction.

Hypothesis—7

"The teachers with low, average and high teaching experience do not differ significantly in the level of their job satisfaction".

A comparison was made to test the validity of the above hypothesis. The teachers with less than 10 years experience were put in low experience category, the teachers between 11-20 years of experience were put in average experience category, and the teachers with above 21 years of experience were put in the high experience category. The results as follows:

Table—4.13 Comparison of Job Satisfaction of Low, Average and High Experience Teachers

Variable	Sample size	Mean	Standard deviation	Mean difference	Critical ratio
Low experience teachers	17	21.35	4.50		
				0.31	0.23#
Average experience teachers	33	21.70	4.81		
				1.12	1.05#
High experience teachers	30	22.17	3.69		

\# Not significant at 0.01 level

As per the mean values found in the above table, all the teachers were possessing good job satisfaction irrespective of their experience in teaching science and social studies. The level of job satisfaction among the three categories of experience was in ascending order for less experience to high experience.

The divergence in the distribution of job satisfaction among the three categories of experience was not so varied.

As the value of critical ratio was not significant, there was no significant difference in the teachers having different levels of teaching experience.

The chi-square test was applied to test the divergence of observed results from those expected on the hypothesis of equal probability. The result as follows:

Table—4.14 Distribution of Job Satisfaction in Low, Average, and High Experience Teachers

Job satisfaction category	Low experience teachers			Average experience teachers			High experience teachers		
	f_e	f_o	x^2	f_e	f_o	x^2	f_e	f_o	x^2
Very poor	0.51	0		0.99	0		0.9	0	
Poor	4.08	1		7.92	2		7.2	0	
Average	7.82	1	73.82*	15.18	4	164.02*	13.8	2	215.3*
Good	4.08	9		7.92	14		7.2	14	
Very good	0.51	6		0.99	13		0.9	14	

* Significant at 0.01 level

There was a significant difference in the distribution of job satisfaction among the three categories of teachers with varied experience.

The hypothesis that "The teachers with low, average and high teaching experience do not differ significantly in the level of their job satisfaction" can be accepted as the three categories of teachers with varied teaching experience were possessing good job satisfaction.

Hypothesis—8

"The teachers with different ages do not differ significantly in the level of their job satisfaction".

To test the validity of the above hypothesis, a comparison was made among various age groups. The teachers were divided into four groups, namely, group 1 (below 30 years of age), group 2 (31-40 years), group 3 (41-50 years), and group 4 (above 50 years of age).

Table—4.15 Comparison of Job Satisfaction of Different Age Groups

Variable	Sample size	Mean	Standard deviation	Mean difference	Critical ratio
Group 1	7	24.29	1.98	3.17	2.49#
Group 2	17	21.12	4.25	0.46	0.33#
Group 3	31	21.58	5.07		
Group 4	25	21.84	3.68	0.26	0.22#

Not significant at 0.01 level

There was no significant difference in the level of job satisfaction possessed by the teachers with different age levels though teachers with below 30 years were holding very good job satisfaction while the rest of the three age groups were possessing good job satisfaction.

As per the values of the standard deviation, the distribution of job satisfaction in different categories was more in the age groups 31-40 and 41-50 and less in the age groups in below 30 and above 50.

The critical ratio values indicate that there was no significant difference in the level of the job satisfaction possessed by the four categories of age groups.

The chi-square test was applied to test the divergence of observed results from those expected on the hypothesis of equal probability. The results as follows:

There was a significant difference in the distribution of job satisfaction in different age groups. The teachers with below 30 years of age were with two levels of job satisfaction, the teachers with above 50 years of age were possessing three levels of job satisfaction, and the other two categories were possessing four levels of job satisfaction.

Table—4.16 Distribution of Job Satisfaction in Different Age Groups

Job Satisfaction Category	Group I			Group II			Group III			Group IV		
	f_e	f_o	x^2	f_e	f_o	x^2	f_e	f_o	x^2	f_e	f_o	x^2
Very poor	0.21	0		0.51	0		0.93	0		0.75	0	
Poor	1.68	0		4.08	1		7.44	2		6.0	0	
Average	3.22	0	177.22*	7.82	1	44.41*	14.26	4	197.67*	11.5	2	136.85
Good	1.68	2		4.08	11		7.44	11		6.0	13	
Very good	0.21	5		0.51	4		0.93	14		0.75	10	

* Significant at 0.01 level

The hypothesis that "The teachers with different ages do not differ significantly in the level of their job satisfaction" can be accepted as there was no significant difference in the level of job satisfaction possessed by the four age groups.

5 Summary, Conclusions and Discussions

In the ancient India when the 'Gurukula' system of education prevailed, the teacher was given the utmost respect in the society. But the Indian teachers today finds himself in a new era entirely different from that of the teachers of the olden days. After independence and the establishment of democratic form of government, the teachers have a new set of ideals before them, it is the teacher that moulds the most precious material of the land, viz., the boys, and girls, in their most impressionable periods of development into required shapes.

Choice of a job emerges as a result of the interplay of a multiplicity of factors. It is mainly the result of an interaction between factors pertaining to the job and those that characterize the chooser.

Job satisfaction involves liking for the work and acceptance of the pressures and aspirations connected with that work. Every profession has got certain aspects conducive for job satisfaction. At the same time it has other aspects which lead to dissatisfaction. Teaching profession is no exception. If we find the dissatisfying factors, we can make them reduce.

However, many are said to be taking up teaching profession as a career because they are interested in it but because they are not able to get any better employment. If one has to be happy in his life, he must be satisfied and happy in his occupation. To get satisfaction in his job, in turn, he must choose it wisely. It is believed that certain personality traits are desirable for the teaching profession. These traits will drive one to be satisfied.

Job satisfaction is a complex phenomenon involving various personal, institutional and social aspects. So the researcher has a wider area in front of him. But, due to availability of the resources and permitted time the researcher has limited this study to secondary school teachers of Guntur District. Of course, in this limited area, few variables such as sex, age, qualification, experience, location, etc., have been taken into consideration.

A summary of the writings of recognised authorities and of previous research provides sufficient evidence that the research is familiar with what is already known and what is still unknown. It helps to eliminate duplication, to fix useful objectives, to form appropriate hypotheses, to draw meaningful conclusions and to make commendable suggestions. The opinions and suggestions about teaching staff given by 1. *University Education Commission* (1948), 2. *Secondary Education Commission* (1954), and 3. *Education Commission* (1966) were collected. The works on job satisfaction of *Hoppock* (1935), *Maslow* (1954), *Herzberg* (1957), *Crites* (1961), *Anjaneyulu* (1968), *Blum* and *Naylor* (1968), *Merill* (1969), *Pestonjee* (1971), *Englhardt* (1973), *Locke* and *Whiting* (1974), *Schmidt* (1976), *Robert* (1977), *Chen* (1977), *Reddy* and *Reddy* (1978), *Davis* (1981), *Karugu* (1981), *Ramakrishnaiah* (1981), *Ahmed* (1984), *Surbida* (1984), *Birmingham* (1985), *Chopra* (1986), etc., were cited. There was a general agreement of these people about job satisfaction: *(i)* It is the result of various attitudes, *(ii)* The satisfied felt more successful, *(iii)* Job characteristics will effect the job satisfaction, *(iv)* Good work environment gives good job satisfaction, and *(v)* Administration, age, experience, job security will effect the job satisfaction.

Hence, the problem chosen for this study was an investigation into the job satisfaction of secondary school teachers in relation to some variables. The variables considered in the study were sex, type of management, location of schools, qualification, age, experience, and science versus social studies teachers.

Objectives were identified keeping the different aspects of the present study in view. The main objectives of the study were: *(i)* To find out the job satisfaction of secondary schools teachers, *(ii)* To find out the difference in job satisfaction of male and female teachers, science and social studies teachers, government and private school teachers, rural and urban school teachers, graduate and post-graduate teachers, and *(iii)* To find out the impact of the teaching experience and age on job satisfaction of secondary school teachers.

Hypotheses were formulated taking the above objectives into consideration. The hypotheses were formulated in null form. The main hypotheses of the present study was that the secondary school teachers are not satisfied with their job.

Stratified sampling technique was found to be the most appropriate technique because the present study involved splitting of the sample into a good number of groups according to different variables. Through stratified sampling only it is possible to divide the sample into different groups and choose sample from each of these groups. Random sampling technique was also employed to select teachers from each group. Only the secondary school teachers who teach science and social studies are included in the sample.

Regarding the size of the sample, 80 was found to be appropriate. This was found suitable because the study involves due intensity and detail, a sample with more than 80 teachers would involve lot of resources and less than 80 teachers would also bring about problems of representativeness. Hence, 80 was considered to be suitable number for the sample. Out of the total sample, 40 teachers were male and 40 teachers were female. Regarding the teaching subject, 40 science teachers and 40 social studies teachers were selected. As regards the management of schools, 40 teachers were from government schools and 40 teachers were from private schools. Based on the location of the schools, 53 urban teachers and 27 rural teachers were selected. According to qualification, 59 Graduate teachers and 21 Post-graduate teachers were selected. According to experience, 17 low experienced, 33 average experienced and 30 high experienced teachers were selected. According to age, 7 teachers were below 30 years, 17 teachers were between 31-40 years, 31 teachers were between 41-50 years, and 25 teachers were above 50 years of age.

The tools occupy a major role in any research study because they are useful in the collection and analysis of data to draw meaningful conclusions. Construction and standardization of a good tool itself is a major research work. As the present study was a deliberate and intensive one, the available standardized tool was selected. Teachers Job Satisfaction Questionnaire of Dr. Pramod Kumar and Prof. D.N. Mutha was used to study job satisfaction of secondary school teachers.

For the purposes of analysis and drawing up of conclusions from the raw data, mean, standard deviation, critical ratio and chi-square test were used.

Conclusions and Discussions

The following are the conclusions drawn from the present study on job satisfaction of secondary school teachers. The conclusions are analysed and discussed in order to utilise them in enhancing the job satisfaction of secondary school teachers.

1. **The secondary school teachers are having good job satisfaction irrespective of the age, sex, experience, qualification, location and type of school management.**

It is a satisfactory result to note as it is also a factor which is effecting the work attitude of the teachers as well as achievement of the students. One can question that why the results are very poor in secondary schools when the teachers are enjoying good job satisfaction. In this context, shall we think that the teachers are satisfied with their salaries, service rules and work conditions? One can expect a good result in any educational institution where the teachers are with good job satisfaction. Similarly, one can also question that are the academic results not the part and parcel of the job satisfaction of teachers? Many people think that any teacher can get job satisfaction and social recognition when he becomes responsible for good academic achievements of his students. In the light of the above discussion, the teachers are expected to produce good results in their respective subjects, if not the whole investment in educational system will go waste and the entire educational system will become a sick industry though the teachers may enjoy the perks and facilities.

2. **The male and female teachers are possessing good job satisfaction and there is no significant difference between men and women teachers in the level of job satisfaction, though the women teachers are having a little bit high job satisfaction than the men teachers.**

Usually, many people think that the women teachers will possess more job satisfaction than their counterparts as the personality of women is different from that of men. As the men and women teachers possessing the same level of job satisfaction without any significant difference, either of the teachers should contribute equally for the upliftment of their student clientele in every academic endeavour.

3. **The science and social studies teachers are with good job satisfaction and there is no significant difference in the level of job satisfaction possessed by both science and social studies teachers.**

The science and social studies teachers are supposed to meet the academic requirements of the students as many students fail in these two subjects of their bulkness and complexity. The teachers, as they have satisfied with their service rules and facilities, have to concentrate on academic affairs to become part of academic excellence of the students and institutions.

4. **The teachers working in government and private secondary schools and with good job satisfaction and there is no significant difference in the level of job satisfaction possessed by them. The private school teachers are having a little bit high job satisfaction than the government school teachers.**

It is very interesting to say that the teachers working in government and private schools are having the same level of job satisfaction though the service rules, the working conditions and the management procedures differ significantly from one management to the other. It is a million dollar question that why the government schools are becoming zeroes and the private schools are becoming heroes in academic affairs? Hence, it is the responsibility of the teachers working under different managements to strive hard for realizing the goals of education, and aims and objectives of the courses under implementation.

5. **The teachers working in rural and urban secondary school are with good job satisfaction and there is no significant difference in the level of job satisfaction possessed by the rural and urban teachers.**

It is surprising to have this type of job satisfaction by the rural and urban teachers as the living conditions and the infrastructural facilities of the institutions differ significantly. When the rural and urban teachers are possessing the same level of job satisfaction, why the urban students are surpassing the rural ones in physical, psychological and academic aspects? So, it is the obligation and duty of the teachers to make the rural students complete in every aspect with the urban students. Then only the rural students will find place on par with urban students in education, employment and achievement.

6. **The Graduate and Post-graduate Teachers are with good job satisfaction and there is no significant difference in the level of job satisfaction possessed by the Graduate and Post-graduate teachers.**

It is a good sign that the post-graduate teachers are also having good job satisfaction on par with the Graduate teachers as they are working with the graduates with Post-graduate degrees. In many occasions, the over qualification is developing frustration because of various reasons, but, here it doesn't have any significant influence on the job satisfaction. As the schools are with a combination of Graduate and Post-graduate teachers, the whole teaching community should put their efforts collectively to enhance the achievement of educational goals by utilizing their academic and professional qualifications.

7. **The secondary school teachers with varying teaching experience are with good job satisfaction and there is no significant difference in the level**

of job satisfaction possessed by the teachers with less than 10 years experience, experience from 11 to 20 years, and more than 20 years experience.

This result is a contradiction to the proverb *"practice makes a man perfect"*. It is a noted concept that the experience helps a professional in attaining higher levels of job satisfaction as the experience helps in doing things perfectly in lesser time and with little effort. As the teachers with varying experience are enjoying the same level of job satisfaction, the teachers have to render their services utilizing their experience in realising the aims and objectives of their respective subjects, and the goals of the courses.

8. **The secondary school teachers with different ages and with good job satisfaction on the whole and statistically there is no significant difference in the level of job satisfaction possessed by the four age groups. But, the teachers less than 30 years of age are with very good job satisfaction while the rest of the groups 31-40 years of age, 41-50 years of age and above 50 years of age possess good job satisfaction.**

It is interesting to note that the newly recruited teachers are with very good job satisfaction when compared with the teachers having a long age and lengthy service. This may be due to satisfaction with rules and remuneration, ambitions and aspirations, initial cult in teaching, and the need for social recognition felt by the newly recruited teachers. This result also states that the aspirations and expectations of the aged teachers are more than the newly recruited young teachers. Whatever the level of job satisfaction possessed by different age groups, the teachers are supposed to contribute their best for the benefit of the student community as long as they stay in the arena of instruction.

"It should be the ultimate goal of the teachers to make the students settle well in their lives with utmost satisfaction".

Suggestions for Further Research

In the light of the present research and its results, it is suggested to undertake the following studies in a methodical way and with wider approach in order to bring into focus the variables and areas which were not incorporated in this study.

1. Studies may be taken up to study the job satisfaction of teachers working in primary schools and senior secondary schools.

2. Studies may be taken up to identify the psychological factors that contribute for job satisfaction.

3. Studies may be taken up on experimental basis to enhance the job satisfaction of teachers.

It should be the ultimate goal of the teachers to make the students settle well in their lives with utmost satisfaction.

Suggestions for Further Research

In the light of the present research and its results, it is suggested to undertake the following studies in a methodical way and with wider approach in order to bring into focus the variables and areas which were not incorporated in this study.

1. Studies may be taken up to study the job satisfaction of teachers working in primary schools and senior secondary schools.

2. Studies may be taken up to identify the psychological factors that contribute for job satisfaction.

3. Studies may be taken up on experiment of how to enhance the job satisfaction of teachers.

Bibliography

Anand, S.P., 1972 School Teachers and Job Satisfaction, *Teacher Education*, 7, 1, 16–23.

Anjaneyulu, B.S.R. 1968. A Study of Job Satisfaction in the Secondary School Teachers and its Impact on the Education of Pupils with Special Reference to The State of Andhra Pradesh. (In) *A Survey of Research in Education*, Buch. M.B., ed., Centre of Advanced Study in Education, M.S. University, Baroda.

Anjaneyulu, B.S.R., 1970, Teaching Profession and Job Satisfaction. *Educational India*, 37, 6, 185-188.

Anjaneyulu, B.S.R., 1971, Teaching Profession and Job Satisfaction. *Educational India*, 37, 10, 340-342.

Apte, D.G., 1961, *Our Educational Heritage*, Acharya Book Depot., Baroda, 145.

Armstrong, T.B., 1971, Job Content and Context Factors Related to Satisfaction for Different Occupational Levels, *Journal of Applied Psychology*, 55, 1, 57-65.

Baldwin, J.M., *Dictionary of Philosophy and Psychology*, Macmillan, New York.

Belasco, J.A., and Alutto, J.A., 1972, Decisional Participation and Teacher's Satisfaction, *Educational Administration Quarterly*, 8, 1, 44-58.

Best, J.W., 1948, *Research in Education*, Prentice-Hall International, Inc., Englewood Cliffs, N.J.

Bhaskara Rao, Digumarti, ed., 1997, *Scientific Attitude*, Discovery Publishing House, New Delhi.

Bhaskara Rao, Digumarti, ed., 1996, *Encyclopaedia of Education For All*, 5 Vols. APH Publishing House, New Delhi.

Bhaskara Rao, Digumarti, ed., 2000, *Education for All: Achieving the Goal*, 3 Vols. APH Publishing Corporation, New Delhi.

Bhaskara Rao, Digumarti, ed., *Reforming School Education*. Discovery Publishing House, New Delhi.

Bhaskara Rao, Digumarti., 2000, *International Encyclopaedia of AIDS*, 11 Vols. Discovery Publishing House, New Delhi.

Bhaskara Rao, Digumarti, ed., 2001. *International Encyclopaedia of Human Rights*, 7 Vols. in 13 parts, Discovery Publishing House, New Delhi.

Bhaskara Rao, Digumarti, ed., 2000. *International Encyclopaedia of Science and Technology Education*, 11 Vols. Discovery Publishing House, New Delhi.

Bhaskara Rao, Digumarti, ed., 1998, *National Policy on Education*, 2 Vols. Anmol Publications Pvt. Ltd., New Delhi.

Bhaskara Rao, Digumarti, ed., 1998, *National Policy on Education: Towards an Enlightened and Humane Society*, Discovery Publishing House, New Delhi.

Bhaskara Rao, Digumarti and Digumarti Pushpa Latha, eds., 1999, *International Encyclopaedia of Women*, 5 Vols. Discovery Publishing House, New Delhi.

Blum, M.L., and Naylor, J.C., 1968, *Industrial Psychology*, Harper and Row, New York.

Browning, C, 1963. How to Tackle the Problem of Teacher Turnover? *Social Management*, 7, 80–82.

Chopra, R.K., 1986, Institutional Climate and Teacher Job Satisfaction. *Indian Educational Review*, Vol, XXI, 2, 33-45.

Clarke, R.L., 1977, Sources of Teacher Job Satisfaction and Dissatisfaction for Senior High School Teachers. *Dissertation Abstracts International*, 37, 9, 5471-A.

Ediger, Marlow and Digumarti Bhaskara Rao, 2000, *Teaching Reading Successfully*, Discovery Publishing House, New Delhi.

Education Commission, 1966, *The Report of the Education Commission (1964–1966)*, Ministry of Education, Government of India.

Encyclopaedia of Educational Research., Vol. 4, 1903–1908, 1982, The Free Press, New York.

Gandhi, K.A., 1982, Personality Characteristics of Teaching Staff and Organisational Climate of Schools. *Experiments in Education*, 10, 6, 110-116.

Gangappa, M.A., Professional Status of a Teacher, *Educational India*, 36, 188-190.

Grewal, P.S., 1990, *Methods of Statistical Analysis*, 2nd Sterling Publishers Pvt. Ltd., New Delhi.

Gupta, A., 1973 Teachers—Their Changing Roles, *N.I.E., Journal*, 4, 48-50.

Hoppock, R., 1935, *Job Satisfaction*, Harper and Bros., New York.

Hulin, C.L., and Smith, P.C., 1984, Sex Differences in Job Satisfaction, *Journal of Applied Psychology*, 48, 2, 88-92.

Karugu, G.K., 1981, An Investigation of Job Satisfaction—Dissatisfaction Among Elementary School Teachers and

Head Teachers in Nairobi, Kenya, and a Comparison of Their Perceptions of Fourteen Selected Job Factors from Herzberg's Two-factor Theory. *Dissertation Abstracts International*, 42 1, 38-A.

Kuhn, B.J., 1982, Teacher Personality Type and Job Satisfaction, *Dissertation Abstracts International*, 43, 1, 104-A.

Locke, E.A., 1969, What is Job Satisfaction? *Organisational Behaviour and Human Performance*, 4, 309-336.

Marja, Talvi and Digumarti Bhaskara Rao, eds., 1996, *Educational Leadership and Social Changes*. Discovery Publishing House, New Delhi.

Mukherji, R.K., 1947, *Ancient Indian Education*. MacMillan and Co., London, 236.

Mukherji, S.N., 1957, *Education in India: Today and Tomorrow*, Acharya Book Depot, Baroda.

Mukherji, S.N., 1968, *Education of Teacher in India*, S. Chand and Co., India.

Neeraja Dwivedi, 1977, A Study of the Effect of Financial Incentives on Job Satisfaction of Blue Collar Workers, *Indian Educational Review*, 12. 1, 49-76.

Neeraja Dwivedi and Pestonjee, D.M., 1975, Socio-personal Correlates of Job Satisfaction, *Psychological Studies*, 20, 2, 30-49.

Perumal, V., 1969, Teacher's Status, *The Education Quarterly*, 21, 15-18.

Pestonjee, D.M., 1971, Effect of Financial Incentives on Job Satisfaction, *Indian Journal of Applied Psychology* 8, 47-49.

Ramakrishnaiah, D. and Digumarti Bhaskara Rao, 1998, *Job Satisfaction of College Teachers*. Discovery Publishing House, New Delhi.

Rathaiah, Lavu and Digumarti Bhaskara Rao, eds., 1996, *International Innovations in Education*, Discovery Publishing House, New Delhi.

Rathaiah, Lavu and Digumarti Bhaskara Rao, 1998, *Achievement Correlates*, Discovery Publishing House, New Delhi.

Secondary Education Commission, 1954, *The Report of the Secondary Education Commission*, Ministry of Education, Government of India.

Smith, D.B., and Plant, W.T., 1982, Sex Differences in the Job Satisfaction of University Professors, *Journal of Applied Psychology*, 67, 2, 249, 251.

Surbida, M.M., 1984, A Study of the Job Satisfaction of Elementary Principals, *Dissertation Abstracts International*, 45, 3, 1010-A.

University Education Commission, 1948, *The Report of the University Education Commission*, Ministry of Education, Government of India.

Venkatarami Reddy, A. and O. Babjan, 1980, Why do Teachers Working in Government and Private Schools Differ in the Level of Their Job Satisfaction? *Journal of Educational Research and Extension*, 17, 65 to 74.

Venkatarami Reddy, A. and N. Krishna Reddy, 1978, Job Satisfaction of Teacher Working Under Different Managements, *The Education Quarterly*. 30, 28-29.

Venkatarami Reddy, A and D. Ramakrishnaiah, 1981, Job Satisfaction of College Teachers, *Journal of Education and Psychology*, Vol. 38, 4, 211-218.

Additional Reading

Bhaskara Rao, Digumarti (1994). *Scientific Aptitude*. New Delhi: Ashish Publishing House. pp: 100. Rs. 100. ISBN 81-7024-658-X.

Bhaskara Rao, Digumarti (1995). *Animal Kingdom*. New Delhi: Discovery Publishing House. pp: 135. Rs. 200. ISBN 81-7141-274-2.

Bhaskara Rao, Digumarti (1995). *Batracology*. New Delhi: Discovery Publishing House. pp: 174. Rs. 250 ISBN 81-7141-279-3.

Bhaskara Rao, Digumarti (1996). *Scientific Attitude vis-a-vis Scientific Aptitude*. New Delhi: Discovery Publishing House. pp: 143 Rs. 275. ISBN 81-7141-308-0.

Bhaskara Rao, Digumarti, ed. (1996). *Encyclopaedia of Education For All*, 5 Vols. New Delhi: APH Publishing Corporation. pp: 1460. Rs. 3000. ISBN 81-7024-759-4. (set).

Vol. I *Education For All:* The World Conference pp: 440. ISBN 81-7024-760-8.

Vol. II *Education For All:* The EPA-9 Summit. pp: 340. ISBN 81-7024-761-6.

Vol. III *Education For All:* Quality Education For All. pp: 250. ISBN 81-7024-762-4.

Vol. IV *Education For All:* Planning and Monitoring. pp: 170. ISBN 81-7024-763-2.

Vol. V *Education For All:* The Indian Scenario. pp: 260. ISBN 81-7024-764-0.

Bhaskara Rao, Digumarti, ed. (1996). *Global Perceptions on Peace Education*, 3 Vols. New Delhi: Discovery Publishing House. pp: 980 Rs. 1800. ISBN 81-7141-319-6.

Bhaskara Rao, Digumarti, ed. (1996). *National Policy on Education,* 2 Vols. New Delhi: Anmol Publications Pvt. Ltd. pp: 710. Rs. 1000. ISBN 81-7488-323-1.

Bhaskara Rao, Digumarti, ed. (1997). *Care the Child*, 2 Vols. New Delhi: Discovery Publishing House. pp: 616. Rs. 1000. ISBN 81-7141-394-3.

Bhaskara Rao, Digumarti, ed. (1997). *Education for the 21st Century*. New Delhi: Discovery Publishing House. pp: 288. Rs. 500. ISBN 81-7141-389-7.

Bhaskara Rao, Digumarti, ed. (1997). *Reflections on Scientific Attitude*. New Delhi: Discovery Publishing House. pp: 310. Rs. 500. ISBN 81-7141-328-5.

Bhaskara Rao, Digumarti (1997). *Scientific Attitude*. New Delhi: Discovery Publishing House. pp: 120. Rs. 225. ISBN 81-7141-381-1.

Bhaskara Rao, Digumarti, ed. (1997). *Success Story of a Primary Education Project*. New Delhi: APH Publishing Corporation. pp: 260. Rs. 400. ISBN 81-7024-850-7.

Bhaskara Rao, Digumarti, ed. (1997) *World Food Summit*. New Delhi: Discovery Publishing House. pp: 153. Rs. 300. ISBN 81-7141-386-2.

Bhaskara Rao, Digumarti, ed. (1998). *Adolescence Education*. New Delhi: Discovery Publishing House. pp: 238. Rs. 350. ISBN 81-7141-432-X.

Bhaskara Rao, Digumarti, ed. (1998). *Community and School Nutrition Education*. New Delhi: Discovery Publishing House. pp: 425. Rs. 650. ISBN 81-7141-435-4.

Bhaskara Rao, Digumarti, ed. (1998). *District Primary Education Programme*. New Delhi: Discovery Publishing House. pp: 506. Rs. 650. ISBN 81-7141-396-X.

Bhaskara Rao, Digumarti, ed. (1998). *Earth Summit*, 2 Vols. New Delhi: Discovery Publishing House. pp: 930. Rs. 1500. ISBN 81-7141-435-4.

Bhaskara Rao, Digumarti, ed. (1998). *National Policy on Education: Towards an Enlightened and Humane Society*. New Delhi: Discovery Publishing House. pp: 542. Rs. 860. ISBN 81-7141-426-5.

Bhaskara Rao, Digumarti, ed. (1998). *Reforming School Education*. New Delhi: Discovery Publishing House. pp: 575. Rs. 750. ISBN 81-7141-403-6.

Bhaskara Rao, Digumarti, ed. (1998). *Teacher Education in India*. New Delhi: Discovery Publishing House. pp: 424. Rs. 600. ISBN 81-7141-406-0.

Bhaskara Rao, Digumarti, ed. (1998). *World Summit for Social Development*. New Delhi: Discovery Publishing House. pp: 278. Rs. 450. ISBN 81-7141-420-6.

Bhaskara Rao, Digumarti, ed. (2000). *Education For All: Achieving the Goal*. 3 Vols. New Delhi: APH Publishing Corporation. pp: 930. Rs. 2000. ISBN 81-7648-152-1.

Vol. I *The Global Consensus*. pp: 285. ISBN 81-7648-153-X.

Vol. II *Mid-Decade Review Reports of Regional Seminars*. pp: 198. ISBN 81-7648-154-8.

Vol. III *Issues and Trends*. pp: 346. ISBN 81-7648-155-6.

Bhaskara Rao, Digumarti, ed. (2000). *International Encyclopaedia of AIDS*, 11 Vols. in 13 parts. New Delhi: Discovery Publishing House. pp: 3676. Rs. 7500. ISBN 81-7141-465-6 (set).

Vol. 1 *Introduction to HIV/AIDS*. pp: 246. Rs. 500. ISBN 81-7141-523-7.

Vol. 2 *HIV/AIDS—Issues and Challenges*, 2 parts. pp: 805. Rs. 1700. ISBN 81-7141-524-5.

Vol. 3 *HIV/AIDS—Socio Economic Realities*. pp: 436. Rs. 900. ISBN 81-7141-525-3.

Vol. 4 *HIV/AIDS Law Ethics and Human Rights*, 2 parts. pp: 859. Rs. 1800. ISBN 81-7141-526-1.

Vol. 5 *AIDS and NGOs*. pp: 215. Rs. 450 ISBN 81-7141-527-X.

Vol. 6 *Aids and Home Care* pp: 183. Rs. 400 ISBN 81-7141-528-8.

Vol. 7 *STD Case Management* pp: 223. Rs. 475 ISBN 81-7141-529-6.

Vol. 8 *HIV Prevention and Care—Teaching Modules for Nurses and Midwives*. pp: 125. Rs. 275. ISBN 81-7141-530-X.

Vol. 9 *HIV/AIDS Prevention Education for Educational Institutions*. pp: 75. Rs. 150. ISBN 81-7141-531-8.

Vol. 10 *Instructional Modules for AIDS Education*. pp: 111. Rs. 250. ISBN 81-7141-532-6.

Vol. 11 *School Health Education to Prevent AIDS and STD—A Package for Curriculum Planners*. pp: 298. Rs. 600. ISBN 81-7141-533-4.

Bhaskara Rao, Digumarti, ed. (2000). *International Encyclopaedia of Science and Technology Education*. 11 Volumes. New Delhi: Discovery Publishing House. pp: 4892. Rs. 8500. ISBN 81-7141-548-2 (set).

Vol. 1 *Science and Technology Education*. pp: 557. Rs. 975 ISBN 81-7141-568-7.

Vol. 2 *Science Education in Developing Countries*. pp: 334. Rs. 600 ISBN 81-7141-570-9.

Vol. 3 *Organisational Structure of Science*. pp: 334. Rs. 600. ISBN 81-7141-570-9.

Vol. 4 *Science Education in Asia and the Pacific*. pp: 429. Rs. 750 ISBN 81-7141-571-7.

Vol. 5 *Science and Technology Education For All*. pp: 464. Rs. 800 ISBN 81-7141-572-5.

Vol. 6 *Values, Ethics, Talent and Girls in Science and Technology Education*. pp: 463. Rs. 800 ISBN 81-7141-573-3.

Vol. 7 *Popularization of Science and Technology Education*. pp. 334. Rs. 600. ISBN 81-7141-574-1.

Vol. 8 *Science, Power and Society*. pp: 357. Rs. 625 ISBN 81-7141-575-X.

Vol. 9 *Information Technology*. pp: 442. Rs. 775. ISBN 81-7141-576-8.

Vol. 10 *Teacher Training in Science and Technology Education*. pp: 536. Rs. 975. ISBN 81-7141-577-6.

Vol. 11 *Science, Technology and Society:* A Curriculum Framework. pp: 642. Rs. 1000. ISBN 81-7141-578-4.

Bhaskara Rao, Digumarti, ed. (2001). *Distance Education in Different Countries*. New Delhi: APH Publishing Corporation. pp: 574. Rs. 1500. ISBN 81-7648-229-3.

Bhaskara Rao, Digumarti, ed. (2001). *Decentralised Management of Education (Management of Education in Panchayati Raj and Municipal Bodies)*. New Delhi: Discovery Publishing House. pp: 116. Rs. 250. ISBN 81-7141-617-9.

Bhaskara Rao, Digumarti, ed. (2001). *Electrochemistry for Environmental Protection*. New Delhi: Discovery Publishing House. pp: 208. Rs. 400. ISBN 81-7141-619-5.

Bhaskara Rao, Digumarti, ed. (2001). *Global Educational Studies*. New Delhi: Discovery Publishing House. pp: 145. Rs. 300. ISBN 81-7141-616-0.

Bhaskara Rao, Digumarti, ed. (2001) *Global Synthesis of Educational Assessment*. New Delhi: Discovery Publishing House. pp: 152. Rs. 300. ISBN 81-7141-613-6.

Bhaskara Rao, Digumarti, ed. (2001). *International Encyclopaedia of Human Rights*, 7 Volumes in 13 parts. New Delhi. Discovery Publishing House, pp: 6500 (Royal size). Rs. 22000. ISBN 81-7141-567-9 (set).

Vol. 1 *International Instruments of Human Rights,* 2 parts Rs. 3500. ISBN 81-7141-595-4.

Vol. 2 *Regional Instruments of Human Rights*. Rs. 1500 ISBN 81-7141-604-7.

Vol. 3 *Human Rights and the United Nations*, 2 parts. Rs. 2800. ISBN 81-7141-605-5.

Vol. 4 *Fact Files of Human Rights*, 2 parts. Rs. 3000. ISBN 81-7141-606-3.

Vol. 5 *Study Stories of Human Rights*, 3 parts. Rs. 5200. ISBN 81-7141-607-1.

Vol. 6 *International Meetings on Human Rights*, 2 parts. Rs. 3800. ISBN 81-7141-608-X.

Vol. 7 *Professional Training in Human Rights*. Rs. 2200. ISBN 81-7141-609-8.

Bhaskara Rao, Digumarti, ed. (2001). *Jomtein Decade of Education*. New Delhi: Discovery Publishing House. pp: 106. Rs. 225. ISBN 81-7141-618-7.

Bhaskara Rao, Digumarti, ed. (2001). *Nuclear Materials: Issues and Concerns*, 2 vols. New Delhi: Discovery Publishing House. pp: 1100. Rs. 2200. ISBN 81-7141-611-X.

Bhaskara Rao, Digumarti, ed. (2001). *World Conference on Education for All*. New Delhi: APH Publishing Corporation. pp: 380. Rs. 995. ISBN 81-7648-274-9.

Bhaskara Rao, Digumarti, ed. (2001). *World Conference on Higher Education*. New Delhi: Discovery Publishing House. pp: 306. Rs. 600. ISBN 81-7141-610-1.

Bhaskara Rao, Digumarti, ed. (2001). *World Conference on Science*. New Delhi: Discovery Publishing House. pp: 85. Rs. 200. ISBN 81-7141-612-8.

Bhaskara Rao, Digumarti, C.A.P. Swamy and B.S.V. Dutt (1997). *Self Evaluation in Student Teaching*. New Delhi: Discovery Publishing House. pp: 762. Rs. 150. ISBN 81-7141-374-9.

Bhaskara Rao, Digumarti, C. Sridevi and K. Vijaya (1995). *Achievement in Social Studies*. New Delhi: Discovery Publishing House. pp: 102. Rs. 150. ISBN 81-7141-281-5.

Bhaskara Rao, Digumarti and Digumarti Pushpa Latha (1994). *Achievement in Biology*. New Delhi: Discovery Publishing House. pp: 102. Rs. 125. ISBN 81-7141-264-5.

Bhaskara Rao, Digumarti and Digumarti Pushpa Latha (1995). *Achievement in English*. New Delhi: Discovery Publishing House. pp: 214. Rs. 275. ISBN 81-7141-283-1.

Bhaskara Rao, Digumarti and Digumarti Pushpa Latha (1995). *Achievement in Science*. New Delhi: Discovery Publishing House. pp: 159. Rs. 225. ISBN 81-7141-280-7.

Bhaskara Rao, Digumarti and Digumarti Pushpa Latha (1995). *Achievement in Mathematics*. New Delhi: Discovery Publishing House. pp: 125. Rs. 175. ISBN 81-7141-278-5.

Bhaskara Rao, Digumarti and Digumarti Pushpa Latha, eds. (1998). *International Encyclopaedia of Women*, 5 Vols. New Delhi: Discovery Publishing House. pp: 2172. Rs. 4000. ISBN 81-7141-410-9.

Vol. 1 *Status of World's Women*. pp: 427. Rs. 750. ISBN 81-7141-494-X.

Vol. 2 *Women, Education and Empowerment*. pp: 467. Rs. 875. ISBN 81-7141-498-2.

Vol. 3 *Women Challenges and Advancement*. pp: 354. Rs. 650. ISBN 81-7141-497-4.

Vol. 4 *Women and Family Health*. pp: 470. Rs. 875. ISBN 81-7141-497-4.

Vol. 5 *Women and International Action*. pp: 453. Rs. 850. ISBN 81-7141-498-2.

Bhaskara Rao, Digumarti, Digumarti Pushpa Latha and Digumarti Harshitha, eds. (2001). *Biological Warfare*. New Delhi: Discovery Publishing House. pp: 422. Rs. 800. ISBN 81-7141-597-0.

Bhaskara Rao, Digumarti, Digumarti Pushpa Latha and Digumarti Harshitha, eds. (2001). *Women as Educators*. New Delhi: Discovery Publishing House. pp: 112. Rs. 200. ISBN 81-7141-602-0.

Bhaskara Rao, Digumarti and Digumarti Harshitha (2000). *Education in India*. New Delhi: APH Publishing Corporation. pp: 280. Rs. 700. ISBN 81-7648-207-2.

Bhaskara Rao, Digumarti, and Digumarti Harshitha eds. (2001). *Assessing Learning Achievement*. New Delhi: Discovery Publishing House. pp: 128. Rs. 225. ISBN 81-7141-601-2.

Bhaskara Rao, Digumarti and Digumarti Harshita, eds. (2001). *Energy Security*. New Delhi: Discovery Publishing House. pp: 564. Rs. 1000. ISBN 81-7141-598-9.

Bhaskara Rao, Digumarti, D. Harshitha and K.R.S.S. Rao. eds. (1999). *Advanced Biotechnology*. New Delhi: Discovery Publishing House. pp: 335. Rs. 550. ISBN 81-7141-516-4.

Bhaskara Rao, Digumarti and K.R.S. Sambasiva Rao, eds. (1996). *Current Trends in Indian Education*. New Delhi: Discovery Publishing House. pp: 234. Rs. 400. ISBN 81-7141-311-0.

Bhaskara Rao, Digumarti and K. Vijaya (1995). *A Text Book Evaluation*. Ambala Cantt: The Associated Publishers. pp: 100. Rs. 160.

Bhaskara Rao, Digumarti, V.V. Rao, V.V. Lakshmi and V.V. Krishna, eds. (2000). *Status and Advancement of Women*. New Delhi: APH Publishing Corporation. pp: 570. Rs. 1100. ISBN 81-7648-169-6.

Bhagya Lakshmi, Lingineni and Digumarti Bhaskara Rao, ed. (2000). *Reading and Comprehension*. New Delhi: Discovery Publishing House. pp: 108. Rs. 175. ISBN 81-7141-543-1.

Bhuvaneswara Lakshmi, G. and Digumarti Bhaskara Rao, ed. (2000). *Attitude Towards Science*. New Delhi: Discovery Publishing House. pp: 128. Rs. 250. ISBN 81-7141-541-6.

Devraj, T.A.S, and Digumarti Bhaskara Rao, ed. (1997). *Trace Analysis of Uranium and Thorium*. New Delhi: Discovery Publishing House. pp: 195. Rs. 350. ISBN 81-7141-375-7.

Durgani Rani, K. and Digumarti Bhaskara Rao, ed. (2000). *Educational Aspirations and Scientific Attitudes*. New Delhi: Discovery Publishing House. pp: 130. Rs. 250. ISBN 81-7141-555-55.

Dutt, B.S.V. and Digumarti Bhaskara Rao (2001). *Empowering Primary Teachers*. New Delhi: Discovery Publishing House. pp. 283. Rs. 475. ISBN 81-7141-615-2.

Ediger, Marlow and Digumarti Bhaskara Rao (1996). *Science Curriculum*. New Delhi: Discovery Publishing House. pp: 309. Rs. 450. ISBN 81-7141-321-8.

Ediger, Marlow and Digumarti Bhaskara Rao (2000). *Teaching Mathematics Successfully*. New Delhi: Discovery Publishing House. pp: 279. Rs. 525. ISBN 81-7141-552-0.

Ediger, Marlow and Digumarti Bhaskara Rao (2000). *Teaching Reading Successfully*. New Delhi: Discovery Publishing House. pp: 386. Rs. 750. ISBN 81-7141-556-3.

Ediger Marlow and Digumarti Bhaskara Rao (2001). *Teaching Science Successfully*. New Delhi: Discovery Publishing House. pp: 320. Rs. 600. ISBN 81-7141-600-4.

Ediger, Marlow and Digumarti Bhaskara Rao (2001). *Teaching Social Studies Successfully*. New Delhi: Discovery Publishing House. pp: 296. Rs. 575. ISBN 81-7141-596-2.

Jayasree, Kandi and Digumarti Bhaskara Rao, ed. (1999). *Correlates of Socialisation*. New Delhi: Discovery Publishing House. pp: 160. Rs. 375. ISBN 81-7141-517-2.

John Babu, Ch., T.J.R. Prasad, G.M. Madhukar and Digumarti Bhaskara Rao, eds. (2001). *Problem Solving in Mathematics*. New Delhi: APH Publishing Corporation. pp: 125. Rs. 250. ISBN 81-7648-273-0.

Marja, Talvi and Digumarti Bhaskara Rao, eds. (1996). *Educational Leadership and Social Changes*. New Delhi:

Discovery Publishing House. pp: 236. Rs. 400. ISBN 81-7141-320-X.

Prabhakaram, K.S. and Digumârti Bhaskara Rao, ed. (1998). *Concept Attainment Model in Mathematics Teaching*. New Delhi: Discovery Publishing House. pp: 122. Rs. 200. ISBN 81-7141-424-9.

Prasanth Kumar, J. and Digumarti Bhaskara Rao, ed. (1998). *Effectiveness of Distance Education System*. New Delhi: Discovery Publishing. pp: 152. Rs. 275. ISBN 81-7141-437-0.

Prasanth Kumar, J., and Digumarti Bhaskara Rao and G. Sundara Rao, eds. (2000). *Open University Student Support Services*. New Delhi: Discovery Publishing House. pp: 100. Rs. 200. ISBN 81-7141-550-4.

Ramakrishnaiah, D. and Digumarti Bhaskara Rao, ed. (1998). *Job Satisfaction of College Teachers*. New Delhi: Discovery Publishing House. pp: 251. Rs. 400. ISBN 81-7141-438-9.

Ramesh, Ganta and Digumarti Bhaskara Rao, eds. (1998). *Environmental Education: Problems and Prospects*. New Delhi: Discovery Publishing House. pp: 324. Rs. 525. ISBN 81-7141-423-0.

Rathaiah, L. and Digumarti Bhaskara Rao, eds. (1997). *International Innovations in Education*. New Delhi: Discovery Publishing House. pp: 514. Rs. 750. ISBN 81-7141-359-5.

Rathaiah, Lavu, Digumarti Bhaskara Rao and Paturi Koteswara Rao. (1997). *Achievement Correlates*. New Delhi: Discovery Publishing House. pp: 116. Rs. 225. ISBN 81-7141-385-4.

Sanjeeva Rao, P.C. and Digumarti Bhaskara Rao, ed. (1996). *A Text Book of Geology*. New Delhi: Discovery Publishing House. pp: 320. Rs. 525 ISBN 81-7141-313-7.

Satya Narayana, V. and Digumarti Bhaskara Rao, ed. (2001). *Physical Education, Social Attitudes and Leadership*

Qualities. New Delhi: Discovery Publishing House. pp: 296. Rs. 575. ISBN 81-7141-593-8.

Srinivasulu Reddy, M., K.R.S. Sambasiva Rao and Digumarti Bhaskara Rao, ed. (1999). *A Text Book of Agriculture*. New Delhi: Discovery Publishing House. pp: 296. Rs. 525. ISBN 81-7141-482-6.

Vanaja, M. and Digumarti Bhaskara Rao, ed. (1999). *Inquiry Training Model*. New Delhi: Discovery Publishing House. pp: 189. Rs. 325. ISBN 81-7141-515-6.

Veena Kumari, Balusu and Digumarti Bhaskara Rao (1996). *Operation Black Board*. New Delhi: APH Publishing Corporation. pp: 140. Rs. 300. ISBN 81-7024-711-X.

Veena Kumari, B. and Digumarti Bhaskara Rao, ed. (2000). *Psycho Social Correlates of Achievement*. New Delhi: Discovery Publishing House. pp: 136. Rs. 300. ISBN 81-7141-547-4.

Venkata Rao, P. and Digumarti Bhaskara Rao (1989). *A Text Book of Zoology—Junior Intermediate*. Guntur: Vignan Publishers. pp: 370. Rs. 57.

Venkata Rao, P. and Digumarti Bhaskara Rao (1989). *A Text Book of Zoology—Senior Intermediate*. Guntur: Vignan Publishers. pp: 480. Rs. 68.

Venugopala Rao, K and Digumarti Bhaskara Rao, ed. (2000). *Teacher Morale in Secondary Schools*. New Delhi: Discovery Publishing House. pp: 300. Rs. 575. ISBN 81-7141-551-2.

Vidya, C and Digumarti Bhaskara Rao, ed. (1996). *A Text Book of Nutrition*. New Delhi: Discovery Publishing House. pp: 438. Rs. 650. ISBN 81-7141-309-9.

Vijaya Bharathi, D. and Digumarti Bhaskara Rao, ed. (2000). *Educational Philosophies of Swami Vivekanand and John Dewey*. New Delhi: APH Publishing Corporation. pp: 200. Rs. 500. ISBN 81-7648-202-1.

Bhaskara Rao, Digumarti. (1986). *Dhrushya Sravana Bodhanapakaranalu* (Audio Visual Teaching Aids). Guntur: Nagarjuna Publishers.

Bhaskara Rao, Digumarti (1993). *Jeevasashtra Bodhana* (Teaching of Biology, Guntur: Nagarjuna Publishers.

Bhaskara Rao, Digumarti (1995). *Vignanasasthra Bodhana*. (Teaching of Science). Guntur: Nagarjuṇa Publishers.

Bhaskara Rao, Digumarti (1997). *Vidya Manovignana Sashtram*. (Educational Psychology). Guntur: Creative Press. pp. 434. Rs. 79.

Bhaskara Rao, Digumarti (1998). *DSC Study Material*. Guntur: Nagarjuna Publishers.

Bhaskara Rao, Digumarti (1998). *Upadhyayudu Vidya* (Teacher and Education). Guntur: Nagarjuna Publishers.

Bhaskara Rao, Digumarti (1998). *Vidya Dhrukpadhalu*. (Perspectives of Education). Guntur: Nagarjuna Publishers.

Bhaskara Rao, Digumarti (1999). *EdCET Teaching Aptitude*. Guntur: Nagarjuna Publishers.

Bhaskara Rao, Digumarti (2001). *Bharata Samajamulo Upadhayayudu Vidya*. (Teacher and Education in Emerging Indian Society). Guntur: Nagarjuna Publishers. pp: 256. Rs. 59.

Bhaskara Rao, Digumarti (2001). *Bhoutika Sastra Bodhana Padhatulu* (Methods of Teaching Physical Science). Guntur: Nagarjuna Publishers. pp: 324. Rs. 77.

Bhaskara Rao, Digumarti (2001). *Jeeva Sastra Bodhana Padhatulu* (Methods of Teaching Biological Science). Guntur: Nagarjuna Publishers. pp: 224. Rs. 59.

Bhaskara Rao, Digumarti (2001). *Vidya Manovignana Sastram* (Educational Psychology). Guntur: Nagarjuna Publishers. pp: 344. Rs. 77.

Index